CRYPTOCURRENCY

"THE ALT-ERNATIVE"
A BEGINNER'S REFERENCE

CHRIS P. THOMPSON

Cryptocurrency "The Alt-ernative" A Beginner's Reference

by Chris P. Thompson

Book Author by Chris P. Thompson

Book Design by C. Ellis

ISBN—13 978-1505743487

ISBN—10 1505743486

CONTENTS

INTRODUCTION

Throughout the year of 2014, I have sought to put together a book that helps introduce readers to the basics of cryptocurrency. Many books have been written about Bitcoin on either a historical or technical level. The aim of this book is not to shy away from the basic technicalities, but still avoid the very complicated technical aspects of programming, cryptographic code and so on. Terms such as mining, blockchain and proof of work are described in an easy to understand manner. It is also not a fully comprehensive historical reference of cryptocurrency. Only major historical events of Bitcoin and other coins have been included. Simply put, I hope to give the reader an understanding of what cryptocurrencies are, where they come from and how they can be used. You may already be aware of cryptocurrency or you may be curious to find out what they are all about. It is therefore an introduction or a useful reference guide.

At the moment, a common misconception is held by many who are new to the subject of cryptocurrency. They use the terms cryptocurrency and Bitcoin interchangeably either on purpose or due to a lack of knowledge. It is true that Bitcoin has had the vast majority of attention through the myriad of media outlets across the globe. Other reasons why this is the case is that Bitcoin, as a percentage, dominates the overall market capitalisation of all cryptocurrencies in existence. It is the most trusted, well-known and respected cryptocurrency on the market today. As referred to by the title of this book, there is an "alt-ernative". This title is ambiguous in the sense that it could mean there is an alternative to the current way we pay for things or it could refer to the numerous other cryptocurrencies which emerged after Bitcoin. All other cryptocurrencies created after Bitcoin are conveniently referred to as "alt coins", hence the reason why the word "alt-ernative" is written in that manner.

There are 38 different cryptocurrencies in this book. Each one has their very own four page section. Each page consists of the following:

- The first page clearly shows the name and symbol of the coin. In addition, the logo of the coin is clearly visible along with the official slogan and the type of cryptocurrency is it (e.g. Scrypt proof of work). At the bottom of the page, a block reward distribution schedule table is present. It shows the time frame of how many coins have been or are going to be generated throughout time from the birth of the coin.

- The second page describes the specification of the coin. Ten different details are listed at the top of the page. Other specific details related to the coin in question follow this at the bottom. At the very bottom of the page, relevant useful websites have been listed.

- The third page is almost entirely devoted to a brief history of the cryptocurrency. At the very bottom of the page, social media websites are listed (Facebook, Reddit and Twitter).

- The fourth page has many parts to it. There is a miscellaneous section which discusses coin related trivia and facts. Opposite this section is a list of exchanges and the corresponding dates on which the coin was added to these. The exchange list does not include every exchange the coin has been on. It is also important to note that the coin may have been delisted from an exchange listed. Therefore, it is a list of exchanges the coin has been present on, not those exchanges the coin is currently on. At the top of the page, there are coin related images. At the bottom of the page, members of the team who are involved with the coin are listed, if known.

INTRODUCTION

I have, therefore, purposefully restricted each coin section to a set number of pages. This was intentional as it avoids being biased towards a particular cryptocurrency. It could have been easily the case that coins such as Bitcoin, Litecoin, Dogecoin and so on could have had two pages of history. However, this restriction has put the most important historical points upfront for these three coins besides others.

After the coin sections, I have included some pages which summarise the prior cryptocurrencies.

As some readers may be aware, the progress of this book was continuously documented on websites such as Facebook, Twitter and Bitcointalk. On the 23rd of February, I created a Bitcointalk thread in order to announce that I had started the project. During most of the year, I have posted many updates to keep the community informed of my progress. In addition, I created a Facebook group and Twitter page. Here are the links to those pages:

- https://bitcointalk.org/index.php?topic=483187.0
- https://www.facebook.com/altcryptobook
- https://twitter.com/mrsilvercider

Cryptocurency is continuously evolving. It is unknown whether certain cryptocurrencies in this book will be used by a significant number of people one year from now. Some will inevitably fail or will reach the point at which interest in that particular cryptocurrency has diminished to very low levels. Nevertheless, many cryptocurrencies have the chance to become very popular. These are the ones that successfully develop, sustain their adoption and make the utilisation of their cryptocurrency easy to use by the general public.

If you would like to buy some coins, there are many places to start:

- Bittylicious (UK)
- Coinbase (USA/Europe)

This book has been written to educate the reader about cryptocurrencies. It is ultimately up to the reader to decide for themselves if they see cryptocurrency as a viable alternative to the current status quo fiat monetary system. If you choose to purchase a certain cryptocurrency, please do not buy more than you can afford to loose. Also, if you find the information discussed here very interesting, intriguing and informative, please feel free to investigate the subject further.

FAMOUS QUOTES

"All that is necessary for the triumph of evil is that good men do nothing."
-Edmund Burke

"First they ignore you, then they laugh at you, then they fight you, then you win."
-Mahatma Gandhi

"Conformity is the jailer of freedom and the enemy of growth."
-J F Kennedy

"You never change things by fighting the existing reality. To change something, build a new model that makes the existing model obsolete."
-Buckminster Fuller

"We simply attempt to be fearful when others are greedy and to be greedy only when others are fearful."
-Warren Buffet

"It takes a great deal of courage to stand up to your enemies, but even more to stand up to your friends."
-J. K. Rowling

"Do not wait for leaders; do it alone, person to person."
—Mother Teresa

"In the end, it's not the years in your life that count. It's the life in your years."
-Abraham Lincoln

"Being the richest man in the cemetery doesn't matter to me. Going to bed at night saying we've done something wonderful, that's what matters to me"
-Steve Jobs

FAMOUS QUOTES

"A pessimist sees the difficulty in every opportunity; an optimist sees the opportunity in every difficulty."
-Winston Churchill

"As long as you keep a person down, some part of you has to be down to hold him down, so it means you cannot soar as you otherwise might."
-Marian Anderson

"When people fear the government, there is tyranny; when the government fears the people, there is liberty ."
-Thomas Jefferson

"We never know how high we are till we are called to rise; and then, if we are true to plan, our statures touch the skies."
-Emily Dickinson

"Money is not the goal. Money has no value. The value comes from the dreams money helps achieve. "
-Robert Kiyosaki

"If you buy things you do not need, soon you will have to sell things you need."
-Warren Buffet

"I do not agree with what you have to say, but I'll defend to the death your right to say it."
-Voltaire

"We cannot solve our problems with the same thinking we used when we created them."
-Albert Einstein

"Be the change you want to see in the world."
-Mahatma Gandhi

WHAT IS CRYPTOCURRENCY?

Cryptocurrency is a digital medium of exchange of money used via the internet. The prefix "Crypto" means concealed or secret. It applies theory from cryptography in order for one to transfer value to another person without the need for a third party (bank or central authority) . As such it is also described as a decentralised (no centre point of failure), open source (anyone can review the code), peer-to-peer network. Cryptography has been implemented and coded into the network allowing the user to send currency through a secure and decentralised network. Cryptography also controls the creation of new mined/minted coin units .

It uses encrypted software to maintain a secure and transparent network for transactions, decentralization, anonymity, and low fees

Properties of precious metals have been copied. This means that hyperdeflation occurs as popularity and utilisation of the coin grows (higher adoption). Also, hyperinflation of the supply is non-existent.

Cryptocurrencies are less susceptible to theft whether this be from individuals or the state.

Bitcoin was the first cryptocurrency launched in 2009 implementing the SHA-256 hashing algorithm and proof of work as timestamping. It was first mentioned in a research paper published online titled "Bitcoin: A Peer-to-Peer Electronic Cash System" with the real name or pseudonym Satoshi Nakamoto attributed to it. This paper was published on the 31st of October 2008.

Since the inception of Bitcoin, many other coins have been launched and developed. More than two years later after the launch of Bitcoin, the first alt coin called Namecoin and the first Scrypt* based coin called Litecoin were released in 2011. One year later, Peercoin entered the market as the first coin to utilise proof of stake alongside proof of work as timestamping .

In the year 2014, there has been an explosion of alternatives, each one vying to become credible or a competitor to Bitcoin. Some developers have also openly said that they view their coin as complementary to Bitcoin. Simply put, they see their coin working alongside Bitcoin, but tailoring the coin to be used in different scenarios of payment. Below is a table listing some of the very first cryptocurrencies:

Cryptocurrency	Symbol	Founder	Date Launched	Hashing Algorithm	Timestamping Algorithm
Bitcoin	BTC	Satoshi Nakamoto	3rd of January 2009	SHA-256	Proof of Work
Namecoin	NMC	Vincent Durham	19th of April 2011	SHA-256	Proof of Work
Litecoin	LTC	Charles Lee	13th of October 2011	Scrypt	Proof of Work
Peercoin	PPC	Sunny King	19th of August 2012	SHA-256	Proof of Work/Stake
Novacoin	NVC	Balthazar	9th of February 2013	Scrypt	Proof of Work/Stake

*Tenebrix was actually the first Scrypt based coin, but did not survive. Litecoin is described as the first Scrypt coin to still exist today. Litecoin was the first cryptocurrency to use <u>Scrypt</u> successfully.

WHY DO CRYPTOCURRENCIES EXIST?

In order to answer the question "Why do they exist?", one has to first understand the motivation behind their inception and then future use. One of the mayor reasons why they exist is due to the financial crisis of 2007/08. A growing number of people have become very disillusioned with banking institutions and their affiliated partners in the financial services industries around the world. In particular, the tipping point for many people were the government "Bail Outs" of mayor banks. This was viewed by many critics as an anti-capitalist stance, as they rewarded the banking system for failure. Since this occurred there have been many instances of fraud. One example being the LIBOR Scandal. Some benefits of cryptocurrency are:

- They are a useful medium of exchange via which value can be transferred anywhere in the world for a fraction of the cost of other conventional methods (e.g. Western Union). Only a very small transaction fee is necessary. As a result, it costs a transaction fee of pennies to transfer thousands of pounds.

- They eliminate the need for a trusted third party such as a bank, clearing house or other centralised authority (e.g. PayPal). All transactions of cryptocurrency are solely from one person to another (peer-to-peer). You have the authority to send value across the decentralised network as an individual.

- Cryptocurrencies have the potential to engage about two thirds of the worlds populations who are without a bank account (unbanked). Therefore, it can become a valuable service to those who are willing to utilise cryptocurrency software on smartphones, tablets, or have access to a personal computer connected to the Internet.

Bitcoin and other cryptocurrencies seek to educate, encourage and engage people around the world that there is a viable alternative to the current status quo. Cryptocurrencies are transparent in the sense that, for a particular one, it is known how many coins have been generated in a given specific time frame and how many coins are going to be released in the future. Most importantly, the coins cannot be generated at an accelerated rate. They have therefore been inherently designed to sustain their value over long periods of time. This property makes them an ideal candidate to participate in an economy based on savings and investment for future prosperity. This would also go a long way to reduce the bloated consumerist society we have presently, and so promote long term ethics, not short term greed.

WHY ARE THERE SO MANY ALTERNATIVES?

There exist hundreds of alternative coins. Many of these coins are effectively copies of prior released ones with minor specification alterations to the certain source code of another existent coin. As specified in the course of this book, coins have differing current and projected coin supplies, block times, timestamping methods, hashing algorithms and so on.

Bitcoin is not classed as an alternative coin because it was, of course, the first cryptocurrency created. It paved the way for all the other coins to follow. Bitcoin dominates the space of cryptocurrency in terms of the market capitalisation (the total value of all Bitcoins in circulation) it possesses and the much higher media attention it has been subject to.

Other reasons why so many alternative cryptocurrencies have become available are:

♦ Founders create their coin as a viable competitor to Bitcoin. Competition within the cryptocurrency space is seen by many to be healthy.

♦ Some communities have focused on certain industries, charities, themes and people in the marketing of their coin. Sometimes it is the name of the coin that determines or influences its underlying purpose or audience.

♦ Developers use the source code of prior coins to which they add/substitute their own innovative code. For example, the developers of Megacoin invented the Kimoto Gravity Well difficulty retarget algorithm. This was then adopted by over one hundred other coins.

A lot of alternative cryptocurrencies fail to gain traction within the space. The reasons for this becoming the case could be a lack of developer interest, a lacklustre community following or a fall out between the initial founders, developers and marketing team. Nevertheless, a lot can be learnt from the failure of alternatives by all coin communities. As soon as they see how things can fail, they are more prepared to improve upon past mistakes by others. Simply put, the altcoin space can be described as an "experimental playground" in which certain innovative features can be built, tested and then maybe implemented.

IS CRYPTOCURRENCY MONEY?

Money is a form of acceptable, convenient and valued medium of payment for goods and services within an economy. It allows two parties to exchange goods or services without the need to barter. This eradicates the potential situation where one party of the two may not want what the other has to offer. The main properties of money are:

♦ **As a medium of exchange**—money can be used as a means to buy/sell goods/services without the need to barter.

♦ **A unit of account**—a common measure of value wherever one is in the world.

♦ **Portable**—easily transferred from one party to another. The medium used can be easily carried.

♦ **Durable**—all units of the currency can be lost, but not destroyed.

♦ **Divisible**—each unit can be subdivided into smaller fractions of that unit.

♦ **Fungible**— each unit of account is the same as every other unit within the medium ($1=$1)

♦ **As a store of value**—it sustains its purchasing power (what it can buy) over long periods of time.

Taking into consideration the above properties, it is easy to see that cryptocurrencies satisfy the first six. As a store of value over long periods of time, the cryptocurrency in question has to sustain its utilisation as a form of payment for good and services or as a means to invest money for the future. Some people describe "alt coins" as commodities similar to precious metals.

As demand for a cryptocurrency increases/decreases, their value increases/decreases.

The value of cryptocurrencies, like all currencies, comes from people willing to accept them as a medium of exchange for payment of goods or services. As they are adopted by more individuals or merchants, their intrinsic value increases accordingly.

Some people criticise the volatility of prices due to speculation on many exchanges. Once the utility increases or a large economy develops around the coin, this volatility in price should reduce in magnitude.

WHAT IS MINING?

Mining is a competitive computerised process which helps to maintain and secure the blockchain in such a way as to verify transactions and prevent double spending.

Those who participate in the activity of mining are called miners. They are general members of the public who dedicate processing power (hash) of their computers towards solving highly complex mathematical problems and verifying transactions. This process upholds the integrity and security of the network. As such, miners are described as protectors of the network. Each transaction (held within a certain block) is validated before adding it to the blockchain. By doing this, they are rewarded (as an incentive) with newly generated mined coins or transaction fees. These coins are issued by the software in a transparent and predictable way outside of the control of its founders. A miner can be based anywhere in the world as long as they have an internet connection, sufficient knowledge of how one mines and the hardware/software required to do so.

Miners use GPUs (Graphical Processing Units) or CPUs (Central Processing Units) to process transactions by hashing. Also, Application Specific Integrated Circuits (ASICs) allow miners to use customised hardware for faster and lower power mining.

A miner can choose whether to mine solo or as part of a mining pool (multipools). A mining pool allows miners to combine their hashing power with others in order to successfully find blocks. It's a global network owned and supported by the people who use it. Once a mining pool finds a block, the reward given to each miner is calculated based on the proportion of hash they contributed in order to find that block. Many miners chose to use mining pools as it results in a higher likelihood of gaining a share of block reward.

It has become very expensive to mine coins such as Bitcoin and Litecoin over the last two years. Another hurdle is to initially acquire the expensive hardware. Those people who mined Bitcoin from the start have an added advantage as they have significant amounts of money to reinvest via selling off initially gained coins. As a consequence, miners choose to mine newly created coins with lower hashing power.

Environmentally conscious people are concerned with the enormous amount of energy that goes into mining cryptocurrency. Some coins have adopted proof of stake as a means to tackle this concern.

WALLET CLIENTS

A wallet client is basically a piece of software that can be used on a personal computer. It allows users to send, receive and store coins. Alternatively, it can be described as a means to access the coins from the inseparable blockchain (public transaction ledger). The client cryptographically generates and holds the public and private keys necessary to make these transactions possible. The software can be accessed, downloaded and installed from the official page of the relevant cryptocurrency.

Wallet clients have been developed to work on various operating systems, the main notable three being for Windows, Mac and Linux. Many coins have clients which operate on all three of these, but not all. The reason for this being the case is that some developers working for a specific coin do not have the expertise or/and contacts in order to get all three created.

Clients are constantly up-dated throughout time. This may be due to a trivial logo change on the client interface, or it could be a fix to the code (e.g. a fork in the blockchain) which requires a mandatory up-date.

Once the relevant client has been installed, the user must wait for it to synchronise with the network. This requirement by the client is necessary in order for it to properly function. It has to download the whole history of the blockchain. This process takes varying amounts of time to complete.

After the synchronisation process has ended, the wallet client is ready for use. The user has the option of creating a multitude of wallet addresses to which coins can be sent.

It is important that users keep backing up their own wallets regularly as a security measure as well as having the relevant anti-virus software installed. Alternatively, users can store their coins in physical format. For example, paper wallets are available in some instances and are classed as a more secure medium.

Besides wallet clients on PCs, users also have the option of accessing their coins on mobile applications if they exist. Many coins allow this. These applications can be found at the Google Play App Store.

Below are screenshots of a Windows wallet client, a mobile application and paper wallet:

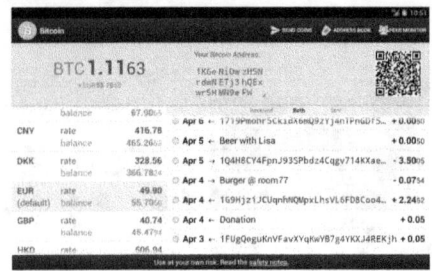
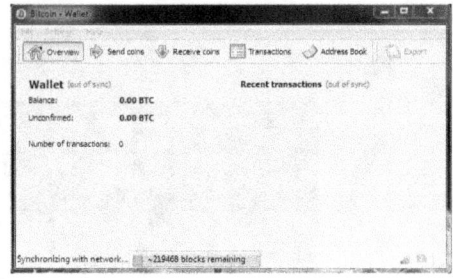

WHAT IS A PRE-MINE?

A pre-mine refers to the initial number of coins that are mined/minted by the coin's founder or developers before the relevant details/code are publicly released. It is important to note that a pre-mine is mined before the official launch date, the date from which miners can then participate in the generation of new coins.

Coins in this book which are pre-mined are Anoncoin, Auroracoin, Britcoin, Cryptogenic Bullion, Digibyte, Fedoracoin, Leafcoin, Litecoin, Mazacoin, Mintcoin, Nxt, Reddcoin, Saturn2coin, Tagcoin and Ultracoin.

There are several reasons why a coin is pre-mined:

♦ As an initial test to check the network is working properly.

♦ In order to raise funds for the founder/developers—these funds can then be directed to future bounties, giveaways and (faucets) and towards promoting the coin socially.

♦ They can be used as incentives to get the word out there and for merchants to accept the currency, and be used as a way to get good programmers, marketers, designers, etc on board.

Scamcoins are known to use a pre-mine as a technique to acquire a sizeable number of coins. They subsequently sell these coins (dumps) after any future price increases (pumps). Not all pre-mined coins are scamcoins. Trust and accountability between the coin's founder, developers and community is the key to securing an honest use of a pre-mine. Many pre-mined coins publish the wallet address in which the pre-mined coins were deposited.

In essence, the founder of the coin must choose the magnitude of the pre-mine so as to please the potential community who will help to develop it. The way in which the pre-mine is explained and marketed is therefore a vital decision.

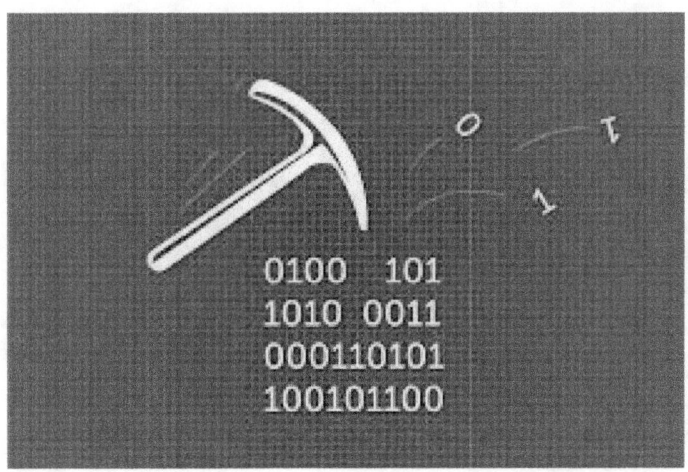

BLOCK REWARD

A block is a unit of data containing some or all of the recent transactions that have occurred in the network over a certain time period. These units add to prior generated ones to form a chain conveniently called the blockchain. Each block contains a reference to the prior one in the chain. This process permanently records the data in such a way which makes it impossible to change or remove anything from the chain. Miners simply confirm these transactions in the newly generated block before they get added to the blockchain.

A block is acquired by a single miner or shared between a group of miners who successfully hash (find the solution) to that sought after block   They receive the attributed reward of the current block (can be a mixture of the newly generated coins in addition to transactions fees) as an incentive/appreciation for the processing power they contributed. This is only the case if the timestamping algorithm of the coin is solely or partially proof of work. Another timestamping algorithm adopted by developers to generate new coins is called proof of stake. Both these are discussed later on.

♦ The manner in which block rewards are reduced determines how the overall coin supply grows throughout time. For example, Bitcoin block rewards halve every four years or so.

♦ Purely proof of work coins such as Bitcoin adopt a simple reduction of the block reward after a certain number of blocks have been surpassed. Many coins simply halve the block reward after a certain constant pre-determined block number.

♦ Purely proof of stake coins award coins to those who stake/hold their coins in the wallet client. By holding coins in one's wallet, the wallet holder is able to receive coins. The number of coins received is based on an annual rate of interest.

Each cryptocurrency in this book, which was or still has proof of work as timestamping, shows how the block reward reduces as time progresses in their respective block reward distribution tables. Next we discuss the block time.

BLOCK TIME & DIFFICULTY RETARGETING ALGORITHMS

A block time is the average time taken for a miner to solve a block. In conjunction with the block reward, they dictate how the circulation of coins grows over time. For a purely proof of work coin, this could be a geometric series as in Bitcoin's case, a varied reduction with Goldcoin or a small reduction of 1% each week like Worldcoin. On the other hand, other cryptocurrencies, after reaching a certain number of coins, adopt a certain maximum inflation via proof of stake. Proof of stake can be active before proof of work ends or just follows on after proof of work ends. It is solely a decision taken by the founder, developers or community.

There are two competing factors inherently participating in how long it takes for the generation of a blocks. These are the overall network hashrate (total mining processing power) and difficulty (it determines how hard it is to find the solution to that block or how difficult it is to hash a new block). Therefore, as more hash power is committed to solving blocks, the difficulty will increase according to predetermined code. This sustains the stated block time of the coin. Coins such as Darkcoin relate the reward per block to the difficulty in such a way that their overall coin supply converges to some maximum if the difficulty increases linearly.

There have been many instances of long periods of bloated block times in some cryptocurrencies. This is the result of a substantial increase in the network hash (overall mining processing power) followed by an increase in the difficulty. After this increase in difficulty, there is a sudden reduction in hash. This leaves the network in a state of high difficulty and low hash for a certain period before the difficulty of the network is adjusted (retargeted) again. Consequently, the blocks take longer to solve and, in turn, transactions are slower. However, over the long term, the block time averages to the stated given time of the cryptocurrency in question. They were victims of very influential miners who used their high processing power on their already low hashrate coin. It is, therefore, a problem with cryptocurrenices in their infancy with low adoption.

A solution to this problem originated with the creation of a special difficulty retargeting algorithm called Kimoto's Gravity Well (KGW). It was created on the 28th of August 2013 thanks to Dr. Kimoto Chan, "kimoto", the founder of Megacoin. It was implemented into the code of Megacoin with great results. Other coins were then encouraged to implement this freely available open code. Over one hundred coins did so.

Many coins have sought to improve upon the KGW algorithm. For example, Darkcoin created DGW.

BLOCKCHAIN

Each cryptocurrency has a corresponding public database of transactions within its decentralised network. The blockchain is simply described as a real-time (continuously up-to-date) public general ledger of all transactions (a long list of all the blocks) ever executed in the history of the cryptocurrency in question. Blocks enter the blockchain in such a manner that each block contains the hash of the previous block. This property makes it utterly resistant to modification along the chain since each block is related to the prior one. As a consequence, the problem of doubling-spending is solved.

All cryptocurrencies have corresponding coin specific block explorer websites. Many block explorers tend to have different layouts, they detail varying statistics/charts and some are more extensive in terms of the information that they give. Statistics include:

- **Height of the block**—the block number of the network.

- **Time of the block**—the time at which the block was added to the blockchain.

- **Transactions**—the number of transactions in that particular block.

- **Total Sent**—the total amount of cryptocurrency sent in that particular block.

- **Reward of the block**—how many coins were generated in the block (added to overall coin circulation).

Many other block explorers list the richest and busiest wallet addresses.

One of the most famous block explorers online is called "blockchain.info". A live feed of all bitcoin transactions is visible on the homepage.

On the blockchain one can also check the activity of each wallet address.

In essence, the blockchain is the backbone of the cryptocurrency.

In conclusion, a block is a virtual unit which holds transactions and awards a reward to the miner/s who successfully generated the correct hash for that block via proof of work mining.

CRYPTOCURRENCY COMMUNITIES

A community is a social unit or network that shares common values and goals. It derives from the Old French word "comuntee". This, in turn, originates from "communitas" in Latin (communis; things held in common). A cryptocurrency community is a group of individuals who have the coin's well being and future goal at heart. These individuals almost always prefer fictitious names with optional corresponding "avatars".

All cryptocurrencies begin when a small group of people, or just the founder in some cases, creates a thread on the Bitcointalk forum. This is the largest forum in the world of cryptocurrency and so is utilised by coin founders in order to announce their particular coin to the rest of the crypto community. The manner in which founders announce the coin on Bitcointalk varies between coins. These include:

♦   A few hours before the coin is launched (ready for miner participation).

♦   An initial following is given the choice on which date the launch is via public vote.

♦   A count down to a pre-determined future launch date is respected.

Once the launch of the coin has passed successfully, the founder and others in the development team aspire to grow the community. This is achieved in various ways such as the creation of an official website, forums, Facebook groups, Twitter pages, Subreddits and so on. Many cryptocurrencies create coin faucets (a mechanism by which users are able to claim free coins from a pool of prior donated coins).

Other methods by which cryptocurrencies gain further traction are:

♦   Coin bounties are offered as an incentive to create merchant services or promotional material.

♦   Coin competitions or giveaways.

♦   Coin news blogs or sites as well as weekly newsletters are available.

In essence, the community surrounding and participating in the development of a coin is the backbone of that coin. Without a following, the prospects of future adoption and utilisation are starkly limited. The coin belongs to all those who use it, not just to the founder who initially created it.

WHAT IS A HASHING ALGORITHM?

A hashing algorithm is cryptographic mathematical code. It is basically the underlying computational language used by cryptocurrenices to function properly. Their security and stability as a form of payment across the decentralised network depend on the function of hashing.

The following two tables list all 38 coins with their corresponding hashing and timestamping algorithms:

Anoncoin	Scrypt	PoW	Kittehcoin	Scrypt	PoW
Auroracoin	Scrypt	PoW	Leafcoin	Scrypt	PoW
Bitcoin	SHA-256	PoW	Litecoin	Scrypt	PoW
Blackcoin	Scrypt	PoS	Maxcoin	SHA-3 Keccak	PoW
Britcoin	X13	PoS	Mazacoin	SHA-256	PoW
Colossuscoin	Scrypt	PoS	Megacoin	Scrypt	PoW
Crypto Bullion	Scrypt	PoW/PoS	Mintcoin	Scrypt	PoS
Darkcoin	X11	PoW	Mooncoin	Scrypt	PoW
Diamond	Groestl	PoW/PoS	Nxt	*	PoS
Digibyte	Multi-Algo	PoW	Peercoin	SHA-256	PoW/PoS
Digitalcoin	Multi-Algo	PoW	Primecoin	Cunningham	PoW
Dogecoin	Scrypt	PoW	Quark	SHA-3	PoW
Fastcoin	Scrypt	PoW	Reddcoin	Scrypt	PoSV
Feathercoin	NeoScrypt	PoW	Saturn2coin	Scrypt	PoS
Fedoracoin	Scrypt	PoW	Tagcoin	Scrypt	PoW/PoS
Franko	Scrypt	PoW	Topcoin2	Scrypt	PoW/PoS
Goldcoin	Scrypt	PoW	Ultracoin	Scrypt-Chacha	PoW/PoS
Hobonickels	Scrypt	PoW/PoS	Worldcoin	Scrypt	PoW
Infinitecoin	Scrypt	PoW	Zetacoin	SHA-256	PoW

*Nxt is described as being an unconventional cryptocurrency. Its hashing algorithm is not derived from earlier cryptocurrencies; it was built from scratch. Its founders say it is not an "alt coin".

WHAT IS A TIMESTAMPING ALGORITHM?

Timestamping is an important feature of cryptocurrencies. They are the methods used to secure the network in order to sustain decentralisation and validate transactions. Therefore, no third party needs to be trusted to verify and then add transactions the blockchain.

There are currently two major timestamping algorithms applied to cryptocurrencies. These are:

PROOF OF WORK (PoW)

- Bitcoin was the first cryptocurrency to use it.

- It was the first timestamping algorithm/scheme to be invented.

- It is necessary for miners to offer the processing power of their computers in order for them to have a chance at successfully acquiring a block reward.

- As the hash of the network increases, the network becomes more secure. As a consequence, a 51% attack on the network becomes less likely because it would take large amounts of costly processing power. This would therefore be very costly for the attacker.

PROOF OF STAKE (PoS)

- Peercoin was the first cryptocurrency to use it alongside proof of work.

- It was independently discovered by "Sunny King" after he studied the work of Nakamoto.

- Users of the wallet client help to secure the network by keeping their clients active. When coins arrive in a given wallet address, they begin to age. If the user chooses to hold a certain number of coins in this address for a minimum amount of time, they become eligible to receive new coins or a stake based on an annual rate of interest.

- It is more environmentally friendly as high power consumption of mining is not needed.

- A attacker must own over half of coins in existence to potentially put the network at risk if they choose to compromise it. However, their high share will also be put at risk.

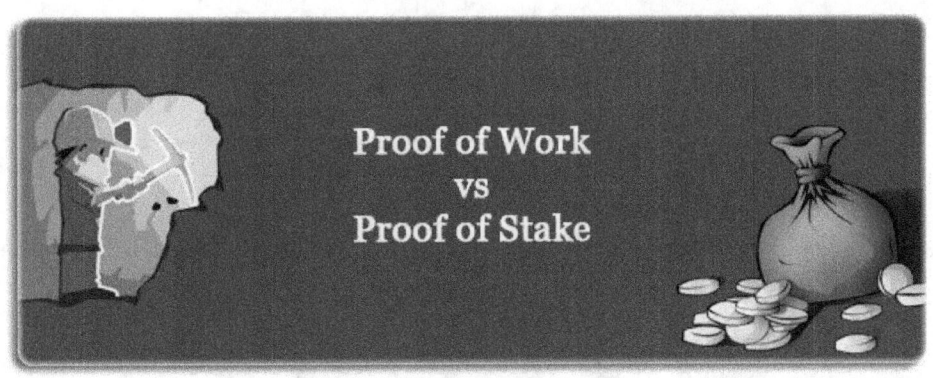

Proof of Work
vs
Proof of Stake

COIN EXCHANGES

In the sense of cryptocurrency, a coin exchange is a site on which registered users can buy or sell a multitude of different coins. Some exchanges require users to fully register by submitting certain documentation including proof of identity and address. On the other hand, a lot of exchanges only require users to register with a simple username and password with the use of a currently held e-mail account.

Before the birth of exchanges, users had to buy and sell Bitcoin as well as other alternatives through forums and chatrooms. This practice was often seen as risky. An alternative practice was to meet someone face to face in order to do an exchange from fiat to crypto, or vice versa.

One of the first and most well known coin exchanges was Mt Gox (Magic The Gathering Online Trading Service), a Bitcoin exchange based in Tokyo, Japan. They began to function as a Bitcoin exchange in July 2010 and then became the dominant player in the exchange market. However, in February 2014, it suspended trading, closed its website and filed for a form of bankruptcy protection. It announced that about 850,000 BTC went missing. A lot of commentators saw this as Bitcoin's demise, but this view was counteracted by many who said that Mt Gox is not Bitcoin. Mt Gox relied on Bitcoin via trading, but Bitcoin continues to survive without Mt Gox.

Further exchanges have been created throughout the last three to four years. The most notable ones include BTC-e, Cryptsy, Mintpal, Bter, Poloniex and Bittrex. These exchanges enjoy the highest trade volumes and are the most trusted and reputable by cryptocurrency users.

It is very often the case that one must possess either BTC or LTC on the exchanges in order to buy a vast array of different alternative coins. This is due to the fact that the vast majority the alternatives are traded against BTC and LTC. The price of each alternative coin is therefore denominated in either BTC or LTC, from which the fiat value can be derived from both the fiat value of both of these. Websites such as www.coinmarketcap.com list the current prices of hundreds of alternative coins. A weighted average price of each coin is calculated automatically by taking into account that coin's price and trade volume from an array of exchanges.

ANONYMITY

The term anonymity is defined as the quality or state of being unknown or unacknowledged. In terms of cryptocurrency, it is the inability of a third party to identify the sender or the receiver in a given coin transaction.

One cannot say with utter confidence that cryptocurrency transactions are 100% anonymous.

Members of the public who use cryptocurrencies do not necessarily use it because it has a certain degree of anonymity. Instead, they are more likely to use it as a more convenient means to transfer value or as a store of value over a long indefinite period.

On the other hand, transparency can be exercised. A user can purposefully associate a given wallet address with the name/address of a real individual, business or charity. For example, a charity can easily create a wallet address to which donors can send coins. By making this address public on their official website, other members of the public, via the blockchain, can keep track of the amount raised.

Developers of certain coins are working to achieve true anonymity. Anoncoin and Darkcoin are strong examples in this particular case.

Many avenues have been used to make cryptocurrency transactions anonymous. These are:

♦   The use of a anonymous routing protocol called TOR. This is used by people to want to keep their identity secret.

♦   A protocol called Zerocoin used to make transactions truly anonymous.

Ultimately, the degree of anonymity is chosen by the individual or group who uses the coin.

CRYPTOCURRENCY SECTIONS

Anoncoin (ANC)

Auroracoin (AUR)

Bitcoin (BTC)

Blackcoin (BC)

Britcoin (BRIT)

Colossuscoin (COL)

Crypto Bullion (CBX)

Darkcoin (DRK)

Diamond (DMD)

Digibyte (DGB)

Digitalcoin (DGC)

Dogecoin (DOGE)

Fastcoin (FST)

Feathercoin (FTC)

Fedoracoin (TIPS)

Franko (FRK)

Goldcoin (GLD)

Hobonickels (HBN)

Infinitecoin (IFC)

Kittehcoin (MEOW)

Leafcoin (LEAF)

Litecoin (LTC)

Maxcoin (MAX)

Mazacoin (MZC)

Megacoin (MEC)

Mintcoin (MINT)

Mooncoin (MOON)

Nxt (NXT)

Peercoin (PPC)

Primecoin (XPM)

Quark (QRK)

Reddcoin (RDD)

Saturn2coin (SAT2)

Tagcoin (TAG)

Topcoin2 (TOP2)

Ultracoin (UTC)

Worldcoin (WDC)

Zetacoin (ZET)

ANONCOIN

"JOIN THE RIDE ACROSS THE ANONYMOUS NETWORKS—WE WANT YOU!"

Scrypt (IP2, TOR) Proof of Work

BLOCK REWARD DISTRIBUTION SCHEDULE TABLE

Block Phase	Block Number	Reward	Date of Initial Block
Pre-mine	1-1,000	4.2	~2nd of June 2013
1st Phase	1,001-41,999	4.2	~5th of June 2013
2nd Phase	42,000-77,776	7	~8th of July 2013
3rd Phase	77,777-87,776	5	~20th of August 2013
4th Phase	87,777-306,599	5	~31st of October 2013
1st Halving	306,600-613,199	2.5	~26th of January 2015
2nd Halving	613,200-919,799	1.25	~25th of October 2016
3rd Halving	919,800-1,226,399	0.625	~26th of July 2018

The block reward continues to halve every 306,600 blocks (~every 21 months).
There was a bonus block of 10.10 ANC at block 77,778 on the 20th of August 2013.

ANC

ANONCOIN

"JOIN THE RIDE ACROSS THE ANONYMOUS NETWORKS—WE WANT YOU!"

SPECIFICATION

Symbol:	ANC, Ⱥ
Launched (Founder):	5th of June 2013 ("meeh")
Hashing Algorithm:	Scrypt (IP2, TOR)
Timestamping Algorithm:	Proof of Work
Address Begins With:	A
Total Coins:	3,103,954
Block Time/Difficulty Retarget:	3 minutes/Kimoto's Gravity Well
Coins per Block:	(see the first page)
Confirmations per Transaction:	6
Pre-mine:	4,200 coins (1,000 blocks)

- It was originally a fork of the Litecoin source code, but has since caught up with the Bitcoin 0.8.5.3 source, and taken its own way.

- Anoncoin supports the i2p anonymous darknet.

- The first 1,000 blocks (4,200 coins) were pre-mined by the developers. These were all redistributed to the community by the use of a faucets, bounties and giveaways.

- The block time was 3.42 minutes before block number 87,777.

- The difficulty retargeting was set at 1,680 blocks using the classic BTC algorithm before block 87,777.

http://anoncoin.net//	(Official Website)
http://ancblockchain.com/chain/Anoncoin	(Block Explorer)
https://forum.anoncoin.net/	(Official Forum)
https://wiki.anoncoin.net/Anoncoin_Wiki	(ANC Wiki)

ANC

HISTORY

"JOIN THE RIDE ACROSS THE ANONYMOUS NETWORKS—WE WANT YOU!"

Anoncoin development began in early May 2013. On the 6th of June, "meeh" announced Anoncoin on Bitcointalk. On the 10th, "dreamhouse" pointed out flaws in the code, which made "meeh" aware that a patch was required. As a result, a new mandatory client was released which had to be installed before block number 15,420. On the 22nd, the Anoncoin official website became available via I2P/TOR. On the last day of June, "BroToxer" announced the development of a new official Anoncoin website.

On the 14th of July, Anoncoin was added to the site Coinmarketcap.com. On the 19th, the new official Anoncoin website (www.anoncoin.net) was created. Three days later, the Facebook group was founded.

On the 19th of August, a client (V 0.8.3.7) was in progress. "meeh", "K1773R" and "BroTroxer" were in constant discussion about Zerocoin, coloured coins and so on. One day later, the block difficulty started to re—target at each block, instead of re-targeting every 1,680 blocks, approximately every four days.

On the 15th of September, an Anoncoin blog was created. On the 19th, the symbol of ANC became Å.

On the 8th of October, a change to the Kimoto Gravity Well retarget algorithm and a three minute block time were announced. Four days later, the mandatory Windows Client (V 0.8.5.5) was released ready for users to install before the difficulty re-target and block time changed at block number 87,777.

On the 24th of November, the New York Times mentioned Anoncoin in an article. Also in November, "Gnosis" and "JackOfAll" joined the Anoncoin team. "Gnosis" joined in order to help implement Zerocoin.

Anoncoin reached an all time high of about $6,892,313 in terms of market cap on the 4th of December. At this peak, one ANC was worth 11.99971 mBTC according to Cryptsy. On Christmas Day, a client was released (V 0.8.5.6). It implemented lower fees (minimum transaction fee of 0.002 ANC) and warns users when they are using clearnet (The Internet which is unencrypted without using TOR or I2P)

On the 6th of February 2014, the online service www.anoncoinbuy.com went live.

On the 3rd of April, a new logo for Anoncoin was proposed by "gostro",but it was criticised for having chains around it. As someone suggested, the coin should represent freedom, security and anonymity, not chains. Also in April, "JackOfAll" left the development team.

On the 28th of May, "meeh" reassured the Anoncoin community that the coin had not been abandoned.

On the 5th of June, the total number of mined coins surpassed one million ANC.

On the 5th of August, "lunokhod2" created the Twitter page (https://twitter.com/AnoncoinNews).

On the 5th of October, the price of 1 ANC rose from about 190k BTC Satoshi to about 386k BTC Satoshi four days later. This increased the market cap to about $1,837,285, placing it 22nd among all cryptocurrencies.

On the 9th of November, "Lunokhod" and "Cryptoslave" joined the Anoncoin development as project managers. On the 27th, Anoncoin was deslisted from Bittrex due to withdraw problems from the exchange.

www.facebook.com/Anoncoin
www.reddit.com/r/Anoncoin/
www.twitter.com/AnonCoinProject

MISCELLANEOUS

Anoncoin is a cryptocurrency designed for the darknet with the ultimate aim of making it completely untraceable within the network. "If the central banking system were to attack and downgrade Bitcoin, they are sure that Anoncoin will suffice as an viable strong alternative."

It is fully "tor compatible" and supports the i2p darknet. By transferring one's coins through the darknet, it is impossible to find out from which wallet your coins originated. Coins are mixed from many different wallet addresses. Anoncoin was the first coin to implement this innovative feature.

The first 1,000 blocks were mined in order to set checkpoints for verification and testing.

They are working on a future project called Zerocoin. This will allow transactions which are not shown on the blockchain.

EXCHANGES

Coins-e (added on ~25/06/13)
Cryptsy (added on ~21/07/13)
Vircurex (added on ~25/09/13)
CoinEX (added on ~01/10/13)
Bleutrade (added on ~24/05/14)
BTC38 (added on ~03/07/14)
CEX.IO (added on ~29/08/14)
Bittrex (added on ~11/10/14)
Cryptex (added on ~11/10/14)

ANC TEAM

Meeh—Lead Developer
BroTroxer—Project Manager, Infrastructure
Geekz—Web Developer
Lunokhod—Journalist

K1773R—Developer, Security
Gnosis—Cryptography, Zerocoin
Cryptoslave—Project Manager, Advisor
original—Cryptography, Zerocoin

ANC

AURORACOIN

"A CRYPTOCURRENCY FOR ICELAND"

Scrypt Proof of Work

BLOCK REWARD DISTRIBUTION SCHEDULE TABLE

Block Phase	Block Number	Reward	Date of Initial Block
First Pre-mine	1	10,500,000	~24th of January 2014
Second Pre-mine	2-140	25	~24th of January 2014
Initial Phase	141-5,450	25	~2nd of February 2014
Second Phase	5,451————–--	12.5	~29th of March 2014

Stage 1 commenced with each and every one able to claim 31.8 AUR. After Stage 1, the total number of coins that have gone into circulation is 4,500,000, leaving 6,000,000 in the pre-mine addresses. Stage 2 commenced with each and every one able to now claim 18.18 AUR. After Stage 2, the total number of coins that have gone into circulation is 8,500,000, leaving 2,000,000 in the pre-mine addresses. Stage 3 commences with each and every one able to now claim 6.06 AUR. After Stage 3, the total number of coins that have gone into circulation is 9,500,000, leaving 1,000,000 in the pre-mine addresses. Since the remaining coins are about 9.5% of the total Airdrop amount, about 3.5% of them will be verifiably destroyed. Each stage lasts about four months.

AUR

AURORACOIN

"A CRYPTOCURRENCY FOR ICELAND"

SPECIFICATION

Symbol:	AUR
Launched (Founder):	2nd of February 2014 00:00 GMT ("balduro")
Hashing Algorithm:	Scrypt
Timestamping Algorithm:	Proof of Work
Address Begins With:	A
Total Coins:	21 million
Block Time/Difficulty Retarget:	5 minutes/Kimoto Gravity Well
Coins per Block:	(see the first page)
Confirmations per Transaction:	6
Pre-mine:	~50% (10,503,475 AUR)

- The block time was 10 minutes and the difficulty re-targeted every 8 blocks before block 5,451.

- Coins mature after 100 blocks.

- The pre-mined coins are being distributed to the entire population of Iceland. This commenced on the 25th of March 2014.

- 320,000 citizens will have the chance to get their hands on around 31.8 coins each. Stock will be shared out among the Icelandic population, making use of the publicly available national identity numbers that are assigned to each citizen. This first stage lasted 4 months.

- If more than 6% of the total Airdrop supply (10,500,000) remain in the pre-mine addresses after Stage 3, any coins exceeding the 6% mark will be verifiably destroyed. 50% of the remaining coins will go towards a development fund and/or towards an Auroracoin foundation formed by the community. The other 50% will go towards a charity or charities, to be determined democratically by the Auroracoin community.

http://auroracoin.org   (Official Website)
http://blockexplorer.auroracoin.eu   (Block Explorer)
http://forum.auroracoin.org   (Official Forum)

AUR

HISTORY

"A CRYPTOCURRENCY FOR ICELAND"

On the 2nd of February 2014, "balduro" announced the launch of Auroracoin on Bitcointalk. The official website went live one day later. On the 4th, the Facebook group was founded. On the 7th, Auroracoin was discussed in a BBC technology article. In mid February, "balduro" assured the community that the Airdrop would be technically feasible. He did this via a statement which addressed certain questions and issues raised at the time. At the same time, "molecular" created a basic block explorer by using bitcoin-abe (http://blockexplorer.auroracoin.eu). On the 24th, an updated Windows client (V1.2.0.0) was released ready for download before a hard fork at block number 5,451. This halved the block reward, halved the block time, doubled the halving time and implemented KGW. On the 26th, Auroracoin was added to Coinmaketcap.com. On the 28th, after a 300% increase within the preceding 24 hours, one Auroracoin surpassed the value of one LTC. On the same day, it reached third place in the mineable market capitalisation list on Coinmarketcap.com.

On the 3rd of March, Auroracoin featured on Iceland's Channel 2. Auroracoin reached an all time high of about $1,026,360,933 in terms of market cap on the 4th. At this peak, one AUR was worth 0.15 BTC according to Cryptsy. One day later, it went live as a means of payment on the merchant consumer platform called Moolah. Commencing from the 25th of March 2014, the pre-mined coins began to be distributed to the population of Iceland over the following year. Each Icelander was initially able to claim 31.8 AUR as a gift through Iceland's national ID database. On the 29th, a hard fork in the blockchain occurred at block 5,451 along with a reduction in the block reward to 12.5 AUR (faster and steadier transaction times).

A Windows client (V 1.3.0.0) was released on the 4th day of April. This update introduced automatic checkpoints and ensured that future 51% attacks were rendered useless. Five days later "David Lio" of the Auroracoin Project gave a speech at the first cryptocurrency convention. On the 25th, AirDrop authentication went live through the National Registry of Iceland. Three days later, it was broadcasted that the first car had been sold for Auroracoin.

On the 1st of May, Auroracoin reached 10% of its total 'Airdrop' distribution goal. An article was written by "The Cryptocurrency Times" which discussed Auroracoin as being the biggest "Pump & Dump" in the history of cryptocurrency.

On the 25th of July, the second stage of the Airdrop commenced with each and every one able to now claim 18.18 AUR.

On the 22nd of August, 3,455,055.4 Airdrop coins had been claimed from the pre-mine addresses. These were now in circulation, 32.91% of a total 10.5 million Airdrop coins.

www.facebook.com/auroracoin.org
www.reddit.com/r/auroracoin
www.twitter.com/auroracoinIS

MISCELLANEOUS

Auroracoin was released as a possible means for Icelanders to free themselves from the shackles of their fiat currency financial system. Once their banking system collapsed in 2008, Iceland has experienced high inflation, currency devaluation and strong capital controls.

By using the Kennitala National Identification System, Auroracoin is being given away at a 50% of total issuance to the population of Iceland, a process dubbed the "Airdrop".

The developer hopes to introduce cryptocurrency to a national audience.

Iceland's Islykill (Icekey) National Registry provides a unique identifier that is now being used to verify Icelandic residency and thus qualification for the auroracoin Airdrop distribution.

EXCHANGES

Cryptorush (added on ~17/02/14)
Poloniex (added on ~20/02/14)
MintPal (added on ~28/02/14)
C-Cex (added on ~28/02/14)
Cryptsy (added on ~01/03/14)
Swisscex (added on ~02/03/14)
Bter (added on ~11/03/14)
AGX (added on ~15/03/14)
Comkort (added on ~25/03/14)
AllCrypt (added on ~30/03/14)
CEX.IO (added on ~29/09/14)

AUR TEAM

Balduro—Founder

AUR

BITCOIN

"OUR FUTURE BEGINS WITH YOU"

SHA-256 Proof of Work

BLOCK REWARD DISTRIBUTION SCHEDULE TABLE

Block Phase	Block Number	Reward	Date of Initial Block
Initial Phase	1-209,999	50	~3rd of January 2009
1st Halving	210,000-419,999	25	~28th of November 2012
2nd Halving	420,000-629,999	12.5	~28th of November 2016
3rd Halving	630,000-839,999	6.25	~28th of November 2020
4th Halving	840,000-1,049,999	3.125	~28th of November 2024
5th Halving	1,050,000-1,259,999	1.5625	~28th of November 2028

And so on...

The block reward continues to halve every 210,000 blocks (~every four years)

BTC

BITCOIN

"OUR FUTURE BEGINS WITH YOU"

SPECIFICATION

Symbol:	BTC
Launched (Founder):	3rd of January 2009 18:15 GMT (Satoshi Nakamoto)
Hashing Algorithm:	SHA-256
Timestamping Algorithm:	Proof of Work
Address Begins With:	1
Total Coins:	21 million
Block Time/Difficulty Retarget:	10 minutes/2016 blocks (14 days)
Coins per Block:	(see the first page)
Confirmations per Transaction:	4
Pre-mine:	None

- Difficulty re-targets every 2,016 blocks, approximately every 14 days.

- A 50% reduction of the block reward every 210,000 blocks (~4 years).

- The reward will be removed entirely when an arbitrary limit of 21 million Bitcoins is reached by about the year 2140, and transaction processing will then be rewarded solely by transaction fees.

http://bitcoin.org/ (Official Website)
https://blockchain.info/ (Block Explorer)
https://bitcointalk.org/ (Official Forum)
https://bitcoinfoundation.org/ (Bitcoin Foundation)

BTC

HISTORY

"OUR FUTURE BEGINS WITH YOU"

On the 18th of August 2008, the domain name www.bitcoin.org was registered. On the 31st of October, Bitcoin was first mentioned in a research paper published online titled "Bitcoin: A Peer-to-Peer Electronic Cash System" with the name Satoshi Nakamoto attributed to it. It is not known whether the name "Satoshi Nakamoto" is real or a pseudonym, or whether it represents one person or a group of people. In January 2009, the first open source Bitcoin client was released and the BTC network was launched.

On the 22nd of May 2010, user "Laszlo" made the first Bitcoin real world transaction by purchasing two pizzas (delivered by Papa John's) for 10,000 BTC. This was when one BTC was worth under $0.01.

On the 6th of August 2010, the only mayor flaw in the history of Bitcoin was found. Transactions were not being properly verified before being added to the blockchain. This allowed the generation of over 184 billion bitcoins in a single transaction. This flawed transaction was removed from the blockchain within hours.

On the 27th of September 2012, the Bitcoin Foundation was founded. It is based in Washington D.C., USA.

In October 2012, the payment processing service called BitPay surpassed 1,000 merchants accepting Bitcoin.

In February 2013, the payment processing service called Coinbase reported selling $1 million worth of Bitcoins in a single month at over $22 per Bitcoin.

In March 2013, the blockchain temporarily forked into two differing blockchains. This was resolved as soon as possible. Mt. Gox briefly halted Bitcoin deposits and the exchange rate briefly dipped by 23% to $37 as the event occurred before recovering to approximately $48 in the following hours.

In April 2013, both BitInstant and Mt. Gox experienced transaction delays due to capacity problems. This influenced the price of one BTC to go from $266 (new high) to $76 before returning to $160 within 6 hours.

On the 23rd of June 2013, the US Drug Enforcement Administration was the first government agency claiming to have seized Bitcoin (11.02 BTC)

On the 2nd of October 2013, the US FBI shut down Silk Road (a former online black market) and seized 144,000 Bitcoins ($28.5 million at the time). The alleged owner of the site called Ross Ulbricht was arrested. On the 29th, Robocoin and Bitcoiniacs installed the world's first Bitcoin ATM in Vancouver in Canada. This made it possible for those visiting the location (a coffee shop) to easily buy or sell Bitcoin.

On the 27th of November 2013, one BTC surpassed $1,000 for the first time. It went on to reach an all time high of $1,242 on the exchange Mt. Gox. Its market capitalisation at this time was about $13.5 billion.

On the 23rd of April 2014, the documentary film called "The Rise and Rise of Bitcoin" made its debut at the Tribeca Film Festival in New York.

In September 2014, approval was received from the CFTC (U.S.Commodity Futures Trading Commission) for TeraExchange to introduce a financial swap product based on Bitcoin. This was the first time a U.S. regulatory agency approved a Bitcoin financial product .

www.facebook.com/bitcoinusers
www.reddit.com/r/Bitcoin/
www.twitter.com/search?q=bitcoin

Logo of the bitcoin reference client

MISCELLANEOUS

The value of the first Bitcoin transactions were negotiated by individuals on forums such as Bitcointalk.

Bitcoin reached parity with the US dollar, touching $1 per BTC at Mt. Gox on the 9th of February 2011.

In the first year or so from its launch, no exchanges existed for Bitcoin. As a consequence, users had to trade the coins over forums or through person to person interaction. Initial users at this time were avid cryptocurrency fans who have extensive knowledge.

Satoshi Nakamoto was the first user to mine the coins from the first block (genesis block).

The first Bitcoin transaction was from Satoshi to Hal Finney at block number 170. This occurred on the 12th of January 2009.

BTC market cap passed $1 million on the 6th November 2010.
BTC market cap passed $10 million on the 23rd of April 2011.
BTC market cap passed $1 billion on the 28th of March 2013.
BTC market cap passed $10 billion on the 23rd of November 2013.

EXCHANGES

Bitcoin Market (added on ~06/02/10)
Mt. Gox (added on ~17/07/10)
Britcoin (added on ~27/03/11)
TradeHill (added on ~08/06/11)
Bitcoin7 (added on ~15/06/11)
BTC-e (added on ~07/08/11)
Kraken (added on ~26/09/13)
Cryptsy (added on ~20/05/13)
MintPal (added on ~05/02/14)
Bittrex (added on ~28/02/14)
C-Cex (added on ~16/01/14)
Cryptorush (added on ~25/01/14)
AllCoin (added on ~27/01/14)
Swisscex (added on ~01/02/14)
CEX.IO (added on ~22/09/14)

BTC

BLACKCOIN

"CURRENCY OF THE FUTURE"

Scrypt Proof of Stake

BLOCK REWARD DISTRIBUTION SCHEDULE TABLE

Block Phase	Block Number	Reward	Date of Initial Block
PoW Phase	1-5,000	10,000	~24th of February 2014
PoW/PoS Phase	5,001-10,000	10,000 or PoS	~27th of February 2014
PoS Phase	10,001————--	PoS	~1st of March 2014

Approximately half of the blocks from 5,001 to 10,000 were proof of work blocks (the other half were due to proof of stake). As a consequence of this, about 75 million Blackcoins were mined altogether via both proof of work and proof of stake up to block 10,000.

Blackcoins are now minted within a user's wallet at a maximum of 1% interest per annum.

BLK

BLACKCOIN

"CURRENCY OF THE FUTURE"

SPECIFICATION

Symbol:	BLK (originally BC)
Launched (Founder):	24th of February 2014 06:00 UTC ("rat4")
Hashing Algorithm:	Scrypt
Timestamping Algorithm:	Proof of Stake
Address Begins With:	B
Total Coins:	~75 million (Max 1% inflation per annum)
Block Time/Difficulty Retarget:	1 minute/every block
Coins per Block:	(see below)
Confirmations per Transaction:	10, maturity: 500
Pre-mine:	None

- Blackcoin regularly has its first confirmation in about 10 seconds.

- Coins within an individual's wallet accrue annual compound interest of 1%.

- Minimum transaction fee of 0.0001 BC., fees are paid to minters.

- Minimum stake age is 8 hours (No maximum age)

- In the proof of work stage, the block reward was 10,000 BC, no halving. Proof of work ended at block 10,000. About half of the blocks from 5,001 to 10,000 were proof of stake blocks.

- Proof of stake began at block 5,001. Approximately 75 million Blackcoins existed when proof of work ended at block 10,000. This was ~25% less coins than initially expected.

http://www.blackcoin.co/   (Official Website)
http://blackcha.in/   (Block Explorer)
http://blkfeed.com/forum   (Official Forum)
http://www.dailyblackcoin.com/   (News Website)
http://blkfoundation.org/index.php   (Foundation Website)

BLK

HISTORY

"CURRENCY OF THE FUTURE"

A Russian developer called "rat4" (Pavel Vasin) announced the coin on Bitcointalk on the 16th of February 2014. On the 25th, the first official website (wordpress) was launched thanks to "Soepkip". "Soepkip" also founded the Facebook group on the same day. Also on the 25th, a wallet client (V 1.0.1) was released ready for download before a hard fork at block 5,001. "CryptoStark" founded the Blackcoin subreddit, the first block explorer went live thanks to "rat4" and the Blackcoin Twitter page was founded. On the 27th, proof of stake began after block number 5,000. On the last day of February, BLK was added to Coinmarketcap.com.

On the 1st of March, the proof of work stage of mining ended at block number 10,000. From this point, Blackcoin was solely a proof of stake coin. On the same day, a forum (www.blackcointalk.com) was created thanks to "thenos", but no longer exists. On the 15th, the volume of Blackcoin on MintPal was about 500 BTC within the preceding 24 hour period. On the 28th, Blackcoin was added to www.coinpayments.net.

Blackcoin reached an all time high of about $30,905,869 in terms of market cap on the 14th of April. At this peak, one BLK was worth 0.94505 mBTC according to Mintpal. On the 22nd, the MintPal BLK/BTC trading pair was added to the site www.bitcoinwisdom.com (charts/graphs) and Pock.io.

On the 1st of May, the first BlackCast (BLK Podcast) discussion was published on YouTube. On the 7th, after 72 hours of funding in both BTC, BLK and fiat, $32.5k USD was raised. This paid for a 90 day PR campaign through the PR firm called "Max Borgos Agency". A high knowledge of crypto, specialisation in TECH PR and accepting part of the fee in BLK were reasons why they were chosen. Also on this day, a new Bitcointalk thread was created by "Soepkip". On the 8th, the BLK Foundation website went live. On the 22nd, Mickey "Vizique" Morris became the new head (Executive & Business Development Director) of the BLK Foundation.

On the 2nd of June, Blackcoin joined Bitcoin and Litecoin as a fully-featured cryptocurrency on Coinkite. This site enables users to send and receive Blackcoin as a form of payment for goods and services. On the 8th, a client (V 1.0.7) was released. It implemented QR codes within the wallet. On the last day of June, the Blackcoin proof of stake protocol V2 whitepaper was released.

On the 1st of July, Steven 'McKie' McKie joined the BlackCoin Foundation as the Research and Development Director. On the 10th of October, he resigned from this position. David Zimbeck filled the available vacancy.

On the 19th of August, the exchange Bittrex introduced a few Blackcoin trading pairs. Some of these include LTC/BC and DRK/BC. On the 27th, "Soepkip" stepped down from Community Manager to a regular community member. He said he will keep supporting and assisting the BlackCoin community when needed.

On the 12th of September, Joshua J Bouw ("Gritt"), a Blackcoin Foundation member, attended the OKCoin/Huobi conferences in China. One day later, the price of one Blackcoin had risen by about 25% over the preceding 24 hours. On the 22nd, Blackcoin was added to the Danish exchange called CCEDK. This was the first exchange to offer direct Blackcoin to fiat trading pairs.

On the 29th of October, Joshua J Bouw gave a speech about Blackcoin proof of stake and public relations at the UROSE Conference in Hong Kong.

www.facebook.com/coinblack
www.reddit.com/r/blackcoin/
www.twitter.com/CoinBlack

MISCELLANEOUS

Blackcoin was created by developer "rat4", with the goal of proving that Blackcoin's way of disabling proof of work is stable and secure.

A Blackcoin news website (www.dailyblackcoin.com) was founded by Ralph. The reason why he started this website was that he wanted to create a news portal on which users can read about the latest Blackcoin developments.

The Blackcoin Foundation is dedicated to safeguarding the blockchain and is actively supporting developers in order to do so.

The symbol of Blackcoin changed from BC to BLK in late 2014.

The BlackHalo client makes it possible to create unbreakable contracts and to participate in bartering.

EXCHANGES

CryptoAltEx (added on ~25/02/14)
AllCoin (added on ~26/02/14)
Cryptorush (added on ~27/02/14)
Atomic Trade (added on ~27/02/14)
OpenEx (added on ~27/02/14)
MintPal (added on ~27/02/14)
Poloniex (added on ~01/03/14)
Bittrex (added on ~14/03/14)
Bter (added on ~11/03/14)
C-Cex (added on ~19/03/14)
Coined Up (added on ~22/03/14)
Cryptsy (added on ~29/03/14)
BTC38 (added on ~05/06/14)
Comkort (added on ~12/09/14)
CCEDK (added on ~22/09/14)
BitsparkBTC (added on ~31/10/14)

BLK TEAM

Pavel Vasin ("rat4")—Founder
Joshua J Bouw ("Gritt")—PR and Marketing
David Zimbeck—Research and Development Director
Mickey "Vizique" Morris—Executive & Business Development Director

BLK

BRITCOIN

"DIGITAL CURRENCY FOR BRITISH INDIVIDUALS AND BUSINESSES"

X13 Proof of Stake

BLOCK REWARD DISTRIBUTION SCHEDULE TABLE

Block Phase	Block Number	Reward	Date of Initial Block
Pre-mine	0-200	1,000 or PoS	~27th of June 2014
PoW/PoS Stage	201-20,000	1,000 or PoS	~27th of June 2014
PoS Stage	20,001-	PoS	~4th of July 2014

Initially the coin was hybrid proof of work and proof of stake. About half the blocks from block number 1 to 20,000 were PoW blocks. 10 million coins were mined via PoW upto block 20,000.

BRIT reached the proof of stake only stage at block 20,001.
5% annual interest on held coins in a user's wallet.

BRIT

BRITCOIN

"DIGITAL CURRENCY FOR BRITISH INDIVIDUALS AND BUSINESSES"

SPECIFICATION

Symbol:	BRIT
Launched (Founder):	27th of June 2014 ("will7am")
Hashing Algorithm:	X13
Timestamping Algorithm:	Proof of Stake
Address Begins With:	B
Total Coins:	20 million (~10 million from the PoW stage)
Block Time/Difficulty Retarget:	60 seconds/
Coins per Block:	(see the first page)
Confirmations per Transaction:	6
Pre-mine:	1%

- Proof of work ended at block number 20,000.

- 110 block confirmations to maturity (for mined blocks).

- Approximately 10,000,000 coins were mined in the proof of work stage.

- There exists a 12 hour minimum stake age for coins in a user's wallet.

- Coins in a user's wallet get a 5% annual stake interest.

- Pre-mine used for bounties, giveaways and competitions, but mainly coin development.

http://BritCoin.io/   (Official Website)
http://britcoin.io/explorer   (Block Explorer)
https://britmarket.net/index.php   (Britcoin Marketplace)

BRIT

HISTORY

"DIGITAL CURRENCY FOR BRITISH INDIVIDUALS AND BUSINESSES"

Before the launch of the coin, the official Twitter page was founded on the 21st of June 2014 and the Facebook group was founded on the 25th.

On the 27th of June, user "will7am" announced the launch of BRIT on BitcoinTalk. One day later, BRIT started to trade on the exchange AllCoin as the trading pair BRIT/BTC.

On the 1st of July, a block explorer (http://brit.coinzone.info) was created thanks to "pinemool". On the 3rd, BRIT was added to the site Coinmarketcap.com. On the 4th, the coin surpassed block number 20,000. From this point, BRIT changed from a hybrid PoW/PoS coin to a proof of stake one. On the same day, an article about BRIT was written by "jdebunt" titled "Britcoin aims to become the leading digital currency for the UK". Three days later, "jdebunt" wrote another article on the same site ("Cryptoarticles"). Britcoin reached an all time high of about $75,557 in terms of market cap on the 8th. At this peak, one BRIT was worth 0.01099 mBTC according to Bittrex. On the 9th, the Roadmap White Paper for July was released in PDF format. One day later, another block explorer (www.blockexperts.com/brit/) was created. On the 20th, the official website (http://britcoin.io) was re-launched. One day later, an article was published about BRIT in the "International Business Times" titled "Britcoin: The future of digital currency in the UK?". On the 26th, "Lee 'MiB' Exley" from England became the PR/Marketing team member (4th member of the BRIT team).

On the 2nd of August, a fiat to BRIT exchange platform (www.BuyBritcoins.com) went live. This allows users to purchase BRIT via instant bank transfer. Two days later, BRIT was removed from C-Cex. On the 5th, it reached a peak in terms of BTC value at 0.01122 mBTC on Bittrex. The associated market cap at the time was about $63,105. On the 7th, an updated client (V 1.1) was released thanks to "dennemann". A new addition to this wallet was the statistics page. On the 11th, an article in "Cryptocoins News" was published. It was titled "Britcoin—The Chiefly British Coin". One day later, a BRIT promotional video was released. An interview with the founder was published on "Cryptocoins News" on the 13th. On this same day, the August Roadmap White Paper was ready for reading. On the 29th, the design of the official website was improved upon.

On the 12th of September, the Britcoin Android App became available via Google Play. On the 18th, the value of one BRIT in terms of Bitcoin reached a new all time high. One BRIT reached 0.01456 mBTC according to Bittrex. On the 20th, the Britcoin marketplace website went live (https://britmarket.net/index.php). On the 29th, a leaflet was designed by "Lucas1981" and a reward was given to him as thanks. This was the first BRIT transaction for goods and services valued at 10,000 BRIT at the time.

On the 24th of October, a Britcoin (V 2.0.0.0) wallet became available to download. It implemented TOR into the network. Phase two of Britcoin development was also announced at the end of October.

At the beginning of November, Britcoin was in potential danger of being delisted from the exchange Bittrex. An average of over 0.2 BTC daily trading volume has to be sustained on that exchange for Britcoin to remain trading there.

www.facebook.com/BritCoinUK
www.twitter.com/BritCoinUK

Designed by "Christian aka Denneman"

MISCELLANEOUS

It was launched with true British ethics and values in mind. Values such as honesty, integrity, accountability and innovation.

Monthly Roadmap White Papers are published. These go into full detail of future plans to grow Britcoin.

UK users can now buy BritCoin via instant bank transfer at https://BuyBritCoins.com/

Their goal is to replace Bitcoin as the leading digital currency in the United Kingdom.

Christian aka Denneman designed the current BRIT logo.

EXCHANGES

AllCoin (added on ~28/06/14)
Bleutrade (added on ~30/06/14)
C-Cex (added on ~02/07/14)
Bittrex (added on ~07/07/14)

BRIT TEAM

William Thomas (Welsh)—Founder
Steven Russell (English)— Coin Developer

Christian Bendiksen (Norwegian) - Designer
Lee Exley - (English) - Media/PR/Marketing

BRIT

COLOSSUSCOIN

"ENERGY EFFICIENT, ENVIRONMENTALLY FRIENDLY - SAVE ENERGY AND MAKE MONEY AT THE SAME TIME!"

Scrypt Proof of Stake

BLOCK REWARD DISTRIBUTION SCHEDULE TABLE

Block Phase	Block Number	Reward	Date of Initial Block
Initial Phase	1-49,999	5,000,000 or PoS	~22nd of August 2013
1st Halving	50,000-99,999	2,500,000 or PoS	~7th of September 2013
2nd Halving	100,000-149,999	1,250,000 or PoS	~23rd of September 2013
3rd Halving	150,000-199,999	625,000 or PoS	~14th of October 2013
4th Halving	200,000-249,999	312,500 or PoS	~4th of November 2013
5th Halving	250,000-(unknown)	156,250 or PoS	~30th of November 2013

Initially the coin was hybrid proof of work/proof of stake.
It ceased proof of work mining in early December and so became a 100% proof of stake coin.

COL

COLOSSUSCOIN

**"ENERGY EFFICIENT, ENVIRONMENTALLY FRIENDLY -
SAVE ENERGY AND MAKE MONEY AT THE SAME TIME!"**

SPECIFICATION

Symbol:	COL
Launched (Founder):	22nd of August 2013 17:27 UTC ("muddafudda")
Hashing Algorithm:	Scrypt
Timestamping Algorithm:	Proof of Stake (Initially PoW/PoS)
Address Begins With:	2
Total Coins:	550 billion
Block Time/Difficulty Retarget:	25 seconds/every block
Coins per Block:	(see the first page)
Confirmations per Transaction:	4
Pre-mine:	None

- Proof of stake minting began 15 days after launch.

- The block reward of proof of work mining halved every 50,000 blocks. Proof of work mining ended in early December.

- Approximately 300 billion coins were mined via proof of work.

- Approximately 250 billion coins possible by proof of stake minting.

- The stake age is 15 Min Days/30 Max Days/0.5% staking reward.

- 70 Confirms per block.

- Transaction fee of 0.1%.

http://colossuscoin.org/index.html	(Official Website)
http://coinplorer.com/COL	(Block Explorer)
http://colossuscointalk.org	(Official Forum)

COL

HISTORY

**"ENERGY EFFICIENT, ENVIRONMENTALLY FRIENDLY -
SAVE ENERGY AND MAKE MONEY AT THE SAME TIME!"**

On the 23rd of August 2013, user "muddafudda" announced the launch of Infinitecoin V2 (IC2) on Bitcointalk. At the end of August, the coin's name was changed from Infinitecoin V2 to Colossuscoin.

In early September, a Windows client (V 1.3) was released. This was a mandatory update that had to be installed on or before the 8th of September. In mid September, "sudo23" designed the first drafts of the first Colossuscoin logo. On the 21st, another Windows client (V 1.4) was released. At the end of September, the total number of potential coins to be produced was reduced from 700 billion to 550 billion. This was due to problems regarding high proof of stake coin rewards. A Windows client (V 1.4.1) was available for self compilation at this time. Several days later, another Windows client (version 1.4.2) was released to resolve network issues and it added a checkpoint to the blockchain.

On the 8th of October, the Windows client (V 1.5.0) was updated yet again. This was a mandatory download with immediate installation highly recommended. On the 11th, the original Colossuscoin logo was created by "sudo23" followed by the creation of the Twitter page one day later. On the 13th, the Facebook group was founded. One day later, "sudo23" launched the official Colossuscoin forum (beta version) (http://colossuscointalk.org). On the 28th, Cryptsy added the trading pairs COL/XPM and COL/LTC.

On the 22nd of November, "Maxpower" compiled the first Mac OS X wallet client.

On the 1st of December, Colossuscoin was added to Coinmarketcap.com. Also on this day, version 1.5.1 of the client was released with an added checkpoint. All mining ceased in early December, and Colossuscoin became a pure proof of stake coin. On the 24th of this month, "muddafudda" stood down from lead developer and handed the keys to "sudo23".

In early January 2014, "Crestington" took on the lead development role to help rebuild the coin. On the last day of January, the coin returned to Coinmarketcap.com after an absence of about one month.

Colossuscoin reached an all time high of about $1,140,333 in terms of market cap on the 1st of February . At this peak, one COL was worth 0.00023 mLTC according to Cryptsy. No history of trading is visible on Coins-e either side of this peak. On the 27th, new "Go Green" Colossuscoin logos were designed by "sudo23". On the last day of February, a new Bitcointalk thread was created by "colossuscoin". Also on this day, "Crestington" announced that the Colossuscoin team were working hard on stability issues regarding the network.

On the 6th of April, the official website and forum were newly designed thanks to "sudo23" and "heat007". On the 15th, a client (V 1.5.2) was released. It was mandatory that users updated because it fixed issues connected to the Heartbleed Bug.

On the 1st of November, "Crestington" reached out to the cryptocurrency community for help to rebuild Colossuscoin. Colossuscoin had suffered with flawed code and missing coins on certain exchanges in the preceding months.

www.facebook.com/Colossuscoin
www.reddit.com/r/ColossusCoin
www.twitter.com/Colossuscoin

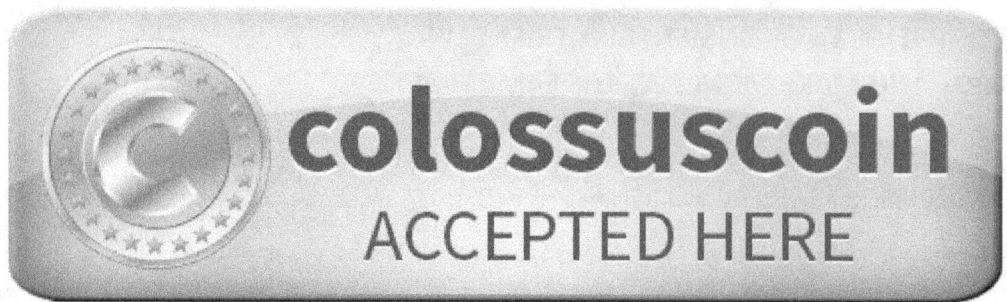

This "ACCEPTED HERE" sign was designed by "sudo23" on the 29th of November 2013

MISCELLANEOUS

Previously known as Infinitecoin Version 2 (IC2).

Taking into account the number of potential coins, Colossuscoin is considered a suitable name.

As a consequence of the immense coin circulation of Colossuscoin, the value of one single coin has been unable to sustain above even one Bitcoin satoshi.

Colossuscoin is the first hybrid PoW/PoS altcoin to hit the proof of stake only stage.

In December, the "COL Improvement Team" was set up. This is a group of investors and volunteers committed to the coin's future.

"sudo23" is the founder of the Colossuscoin Foundation. The foundation helps to promote the adoption of the coin.

EXCHANGES

BTCLTC (added on ~03/09/13)
Cryptsy (added on ~28/10/13)
Coins-e (added on ~30/11/13)
Coined Up (added on ~27/12/13)
Cryptorush (added on ~30/01/14)
Comkort (added on ~25/02/14)

COL TEAM

"muddafudda" - Founder
"Crestington" - Leader Developer
"sudo23" - PR Relations/Marketing

COL

CRYPTO BULLION

"THE DIGITAL PRECIOUS METAL"

Scrypt PoW/PoS Hybrid

BLOCK REWARD DISTRIBUTION SCHEDULE TABLE

Block Phase	Block Number	Reward	Date of Initial Block
Pre-mine	1-934	10	~27th of June 2013
Initial Phase	935-55,000	10	~28th of June 2013
1st Halving	55,001-95,000	5	~4th of August 2013
2nd Halving	95,001-145,000	2.5	~1st of September 2013
3rd Halving	145,001-195,000	1.25	~6th of October 2013
————————	————————	————————	————————————
9th Halving	495,001-545,000	0.019531	~4th of May 2014
10th Halving	545,001————	0.01	~13th of July 2014

The block reward via proof of work is now fixed at 0.01 CGB per block every 60 seconds.

CBX

CRYPTO BULLION

"THE DIGITAL PRECIOUS METAL"
"EARN. STORE. MULTIPLY"

SPECIFICATION

Symbol:	CBX (originally CGB)
Launched (Founder):	28th of June 2013 ("elambert")
Hashing Algorithm:	Scrypt
Timestamping Algorithm:	PoW/PoS Hybrid
Address Begins With:	5
Total Coins:	1 million, 2.0% inflation (0.5% from PoW and 1.5% from PoS)
Block Time/Difficulty Retarget:	60 seconds/2 minutes (2 blocks)
Coins per Block:	(see the first page)
Confirmations per transaction:	6
Pre-mine:	0.94% (% of the initial 1 million coin phase)

- A 50% reduction of the block reward after every 50,000 blocks. This continued and a block reward of 0.01 CBX was reached. At this time there was approximately one million CBX in existence, and the 0.01 CBX block reward initially equates to about 0.5% annual inflation going forward (proof of work).

- There is a maximum of 1.2%/1.5% annual proof of stake interest earnings potential for coins which have been stationary in a user's wallet for at least 30/90 days. In fact, the miners will receive at least 25% of all rewards, while prudent savers will receive at most 75% of total newly mined/minted CBX.

- Proof of stake (PoS) in conjunction with proof of work (PoW) maximizes the security of the blockchain and provides an incremental layer of protection against 51% attacks.

- A linear difficulty re-targeting algorithm is used (every 2 blocks).

- It is a fork of the cryptocurrency called Novacoin. Also based on Peercoin.

http://cgb.holdings/   (Official Website)
http://blocks.gotcrypto.net/chain/CryptogenicBullion   (Block Explorer)

CBX

HISTORY

"THE DIGITAL PRECIOUS METAL"

"EARN. STORE. MULTIPLY"

On the 28th of June 2013, user "elambert" announced CBX on Bitcointalk. A pre-mine of 9,399.88 CBX was mined to go towards development, bounties and giveaways. The source code was also released on this day.

On the 29th of July, the Twitter page was created. On the 30th, an updated client was released. Block rewards were extended to allow for an approximate 2% annual inflation after 1 million coins had been mined. On the 31st, the Crypto Bullion Facebook group was founded.

On the 1st of August, the block reward did not halve as anticipated at block number 50,000. As a result, an updated client was released which had to installed before a fork at block 55,000. On the 4th, Crypto Bullion was added to the site Coinmarketcap.com. One day later, another client was released which fixed an issue with the proof of stake reward system. This update took effect at block number 59,700. This update was also mandatory. Also in August, Crypto Bullion was added to www.coinpayments.net.

On the 24th of October, "MercSuey" redesigned the layout and format of the official website (www.cryptogenicbullion.org). This site was initially launched on the 10th of August 2013.

On the 5th of November, a client (V 1.1.6.4) was released. It enabled transaction messaging. On the 10th, the PoW block reward went below 1 CBX at block 195,001. On the 16th, the market capitalisation of the coin surpassed $1 million. On the 27th, the market cap of CBX went above $2.5 million for the first time.

Crypto Bullion reached an all time high of about $5,822,550 in terms of market cap on the 1st of December . At this peak, one CBX was worth 0.00581 BTC according to Cryptsy. On the 14th, Cryptsy added the trading pair CGB/LTC.

On the 6th of February 2014, "papersheepdog" published the "Open Source Community Development and Marketing Strategy" paper. Five days later, the Reddit TipBot went live thanks to "artifice".

On the 1st of March, Mercury Stills ("MercSuey") resigned from the position of lead developer in order to work on other projects. A new lead developer called "artifice" was hired on the same day. On the 8th, a client (V 1.1.6.6) was released. It incorporated the new gold/silver CBX logo, splash and extra checkpoints. On the 20th, the new official website was launched (www.cgb.holdings).

On the 8th of April, a client (V 1.1.6.7) was released. This fixed issues regarding the HeartBleed Bug.

On the 26th of May, the "CryptoTown on the Ground Project" was founded. It is a project to help spread the message of cryptocurrency through face-to-face human interaction.

On the 13th of July, the Crypto Bullion 1-year inflationary stage was complete. Approximately 1 million CBX were in circulation with a maximum inflation rate of 2% per annum from then on.

On the 11th of September, the promotion of Raizor to the Lead Developer position was announced.

In early December, the name of the coin was changed to Crypto Bullion (CBX).

www.facebook.com/CryptogenicBullion
www.reddit.com/r/CryptogenicBullion
www.twitter.com/CryptogenicBull

An original graphic that shows the original name "Cryptogenic Bullion"

MISCELLANEOUS

Its main feature as a cryptocurrency is to limit the risk posed by customers and businesses. Many cryptocurrencies have inherent volatility for which CBX, described more as a crypto-commodity, aims to reduce by being a safe haven.

It has been designed to be rare in the same way that precious metals are. Crypto Bullion is effectively an interest bearing crypto-commodity.

FiniteByDesign is a merchant that sells T-Shirts and bullion bars.

CBX Core Team Weekly Update is written by "PaperSheepDog".

An article was written on Yahoo Finance titled "The Rare, Interest Bearing, Bitcoin Alternative—Cryptogenic Bullion". At the time, 500CGB=1BTC.

EXCHANGES

Coins-e (added on ~01/07/13)
Cryptsy (added on ~25/07/13)
CoinEX (added on ~07/08/13)
Phenixex (added on ~04/09/13)
Cryptokopen (added on ~01/02/14)
AllCrypt (added on ~10/03/14)
Bittrex (added on ~23/03/14)
Ecoinfund (added on ~24/03/14)
Swaphole (added on ~28/03/14)
PTOPEX (added on ~05/04/14)
Vault of Satoshi (added on ~10/04/14)
Comkort (added on ~27/04/14)
Cryptilla (added on ~25/07/14)
Crypto-Trade (added on ~04/08/14)
Cryptex (added on ~16/09/14)

CBX TEAM

Elambert—CGX Founder
Raizor—Lead Developer
PaperSheepDog—Director of Marketing & Strategy
XORCIST—Peripheral & Web Development

Artiface—Development Advisor/Consultant
LarryHardCore—Senior Engineer (Linux)
Silent Partner—Core Team Member
Ethapus—Core Team Member

CBX

DARKCOIN

"PRIVACY-CENTRIC CRYPTOGRAPHIC COIN"

X11 Proof of Work

BLOCK REWARD FORMULA

$$\frac{2{,}222{,}222}{\left\{\dfrac{\text{DIFFICULTY} + 2{,}600}{9}\right\}^2}$$

The above formula calculates the coin reward of each block based on the difficulty of that block. So as the difficulty of mining the coins increases, the block reward decreases.

DRK

DARKCOIN

"THE FIRST ANONYMOUS COIN"
"PRIVACY-CENTRIC CRYPTOGRAPHIC COIN"

SPECIFICATION

Symbol:	DRK
Launched (Founder):	18th of January 2014 (Evan Duffield & Kyle Hagan)
Hashing Algorithm:	X11 (see below)
Timestamping Algorithm:	Proof of Work
Address Begins With:	X
Total Coins:	22 million
Block Time/Difficulty Retarget:	2.5 minutes/Dark Gravity Wave (DGW)
Coins per Block:	(see below or the first page)
Confirmations per Transaction:	(unknown)
Pre-mine:	None

◆ Launched specifically at 11pm EST on the 18th of January 2014.

◆ Darkcoin is a privacy-centric currency based on the software of Bitcoin.

◆ Darkcoin uses a super secure hashing algorithm consisting of 11 rounds of scientific hashing functions (blake, bmw, groestl, jh, keccak, skein, luffa, cubehash, shavite, simd, echo)

◆ Block Reward (Coins per Block) is determined by the formula $2,222,222 / ([(\text{Difficulty} + 2,600)/9]^2)$.

◆ Difficulty retargets using the Dark Gravity Wave every block.

◆ Superior Transaction Anonymity using DarkSend.

◆ 7% decrease in the number of coins generated per year.

◆ Mined by using CPUs/GPUs.

◆ Masternodes, decentralised network of servers, allows the mixing of user's coins during transactions. This makes transactions impossible to trace, just like cash.

◆ Darkcoin is resistant to ASIC mining because of the hashing algorithm X11.

http://darkcoin.io	(Official Website)
http://explorer.darkcoin.io/chain/Darkcoin	(Block Explorer)
https://darkcointalk.org/	(Official Forum)
https://www.darkcoinfoundation.org/	(Darkcoin Foundation)
http://wiki.darkcoin.eu/wiki/Main_Page	(Darkcoin Wiki)

DRK

HISTORY

"THE FIRST ANONYMOUS COIN"

"PRIVACY-CENTRIC CRYPTOGRAPHIC COIN"

User "eduffield" created the Darkcoin Bitcointalk thread on the 18th of January 2014. On the 26th, "eduffield" created the first Darkcoin block explorer using Abe (http://explorer.xcoin.co/). The currency was originally launched as Xcoin, but the name changed to Darkcoin on the 28th of January.

Darkcoin was initially listed on C-Cex as the trading pair DRK/BTC on the 3rd of February. On the 5th, the official website (www.darkcoin.io) went live. On the 11th, the official Twitter page was created. On the 13th, it was added to Coinmarketcap.com. On the 20th, the official Facebook group was created. Darkcoin reached an all time high of about $4,821,007 in terms of market cap on the 23rd. At this peak, one DRK was worth 0.00219 BTC according to Poloniex. This peak occurred just before Darkcoin got listed on Cryptsy.

On the 17th of April, Darksend RC1 (1st Release Candidate) was made available. A limit of 10 DRK applied to Darksend transactions, plus a transaction fee of 0.001 DRk, at this time.

In May, Darkcoin's blockchain split into several forks. The developers had to alter the code to facilitate the use of the masternodes, which conceal users transactions by mixing their Darkcoins with those of other users. On the 22nd, the DRK/LTC trading pair was added to MintPal. On the 26th, the blockchain of Darkcoin became forked. As a result it was temporarily taken off Cryptsy for a few hours. Also, DRK/BTC was taken off MintPal. It was fixed on the same day. On the 31st of May, Cryptsy added the trading pair DRK/USD.

Darkcoin reached a new all time high of about $67,853,864 in terms of market cap on the 2nd of June. At this peak, one DRK was worth 0.024965 BTC according to Cryptsy. On the same day, DRK was added to Bitfinex, an advanced trading platform based in Hong Kong, alongside BTC and LTC. On the 12th, a client (V 0.9.10.0 for regular users or V 0.10.10.0 for Darksend users) was released. This was a mandatory update that needed to be installed by users before a hard fork on the 20th. This release fixed client forking issues (from RC2). On the 19th, Coins-e added various DRK trading pairs to their exchange. On the 20th, David Reynolds (DRKLord) and Fabian Olesen (CHAOSiTEC) joined the DRK team.

On the 21st of July, Kistov Atlas started to review the code for Darkcoin.

On the 13th of August, RC4 (a version of the DRK client) was released. This update included a complete rewrite of the Darksend protocol, which improved transaction privacy and removed the 10 DRK limit for Darksend transactions. Transactions sent via Darksend had a transaction charge of 0.001 DRK at the time.

On the 22nd the September, RC5 (V 9.13.15 for regular users or V 10.13.15 for Darksend users) was released. It was a mandatory download that improved Darksend thanks to the audit by Kristov Atlas. On the same day, a paper titled "Transaction Locking and Masternode Consensus: A Mechansim for Mitigating Double Spending Attacks" was published. It discusses the technology that, when implemented into Darkcoin, could dramatically shorten the confirmation times of transactions and allow Darkcoin to compete directly with credit cards.

On the 23rd of November, DarkTV went live on YouTube.

On the 7th of December, the Darkcoin Foundation was established.

www.facebook.com/DarkcoinOfficial

www.reddit.com/r/DRKCoin/

www.twitter.com/DarkcoinOrg

Original Logo

MISCELLANEOUS

The main objective of Darkcoin is privacy and improving on what lead developer Evan Duffield sees as the errors of Bitcoin.

The Dark Gravity Wave is a difficulty re-targeting algorithm created by Evan Duffield. It is described as improving upon the Kimoto Gravity Well algorithm by fixing certain code flaws.

X11 is a hashing algorithm created by Evan Duffield. It will take years for the existence of certain ASICs which can mine Darkcoin. A benefit of X11 is that GPUs require about 30% less power and operate 30-50% cooler than they do with Scrypt.

The main objective of the Darkcoin Foundation is to promote and educate people about the coin.

EXCHANGES

C-Cex (added on ~03/02/14)
Poloniex (added on ~07/02/14)
PMtoCoins (added on ~16/02/14)
Coins-e (added on ~20/02/14)
Cryptsy (added on ~23/02/14)
Cryptorush (added on ~24/02/14)
Mintpal (added on ~24/02/14)
Coined Up (added on ~06/03/14)
Bittrex (added on ~11/03/14)
Prelude (added on ~17/03/14)
BTC38 (added on ~25/03/14)
Bleutrade (added on ~28/03/14)
Vault of Satoshi (added on ~10/04/14)
Bter (added on ~29/04/14)
Swisscex (added on ~27/05/14)
Bitfinex (added on ~02/06/14)
CEX.IO (added on ~03/11/14)

DRK TEAM

Evan Duffield—Lead Developer

Kyle Hagan—Systems Engineer

Holger Schinzel—Quality Assurance, Automation and Testing

David Reynolds—GUI Developer

Fabian Olesen—Developer

Fernando Gutierrez—Multitool

DRK

DIAMOND

"SCARCE FAST SECURE"

Groestl Hybrid PoW/PoS

BLOCK REWARD DISTRIBUTION SCHEDULE TABLE

Block Phase	Block Number	Reward	Date of Initial Block
Scrypt Phase	1-386,226	1	~13th of July 2013
Groestl Phase 1	386,227-999,999	1.05	~2nd of May 2014
Groestl Phase 2	1,000,000-2,4999,999 (coin number)	0.1	~2nd of July 2015
Groestl Phase 3	2,500,000- (coin number)	0.02	~7th of January 2044

From 450,000 to 1,500,000 coins, PoS is set to 50% per annum.

After 1.5 million coins, PoS is reduced to 25% per annum (MIN 7 days coinage required)

After 2.5 million coins, PoS is reduced to 5% per annum (MIN 7 days coinage required)

After 3.5 million coins, PoS is reduced to 1% per annum (MIN 7 days coinage required)

DMD

DIAMOND

"SCARCE FAST SECURE"

SPECIFICATION

Symbol:	DMD
Launched (Founder):	13th of July 2013 ("JohnLuc")
Hashing Algorithm:	Groestl
Timestamping Algorithm:	Hybrid Proof of Work/Proof of Stake
Address Begins With:	d
Total Coins:	~4,380,000
Block Time/Difficulty Retarget:	60 seconds/every block
Coins per Block:	(see below and first page)
Confirmations per Transaction:	6
Pre-mine:	None

- During its Scrypt proof of work mining phase, DMD was mined at a linear rate of 1,500 coins per day including bonus blocks. Everyday there were ten bonus blocks of 2 DMD, three super blocks of 8 DMD and 1 mega block of 30 DMD. It used the random block feature from Luckycoin, but does not now.

- Mined blocks mature after 200 minutes.

- Diamond is an ASIC resistant Groestl coin. It was initially launched as a Scrypt coin.

- Transition to Groestl occurred as prevention from Scrypt ASICs potentially attacking the network.

- Diamond wallet supports transaction comments, coin control and fast index.

- During the PoW Groestl phase 1 mining process, 1 DMD was rewarded to the miner and 0.05 DMD went to support the coin.

- The block time during proof of stake is now 600 seconds.

- Proof of stake (by design) will gradually become the main source of DMDs.

- Diamond Coin Foundation is funded by contributions of 0.05 DMD that are added on top of the mining reward blocks. Therefore, about 72 coins daily help with Diamond sustainability.

http://bit.diamonds/	(Official Website)
http://diamond.danbo.bg:2750/chain/Diamond	(Block Explorer)
http://bit.diamonds/community/	(Official Forum)

DMD

HISTORY

"SCARCE FAST SECURE"

On the 13th of July 2013, user "JohnLuc" announced the coin on Bitcointalk. Ten days later, it was listed on the exchange Coins-e as the trading pair DMD/BTC. However, trading ceased straight after its introduction due to the platform's inability to process deposits. They reactivated trading two days later. On the 28th, a client (V 1.1) was released. It introduced new checkpoints for higher security. It was not mandatory, but highly recommended that users updated.

In the months August to November, the developers of the coin went quiet. A new user called "zuper" and other developers helped to revive the community.

The developers compiled a new client (V 1.0.1) on the 1st of December. On the 13th, "Tripmode" created the first Diamond block explorer. In mid December, the Diamond blockchain forked (51% attack) which meant the coin could not be mined. Cryptsy suspended trading of the coin until the developers came up with a fix. A wallet was released (V 1.0.2) on the 16th by new developers who rescued the coin and announced the official takeover of Diamond by creating a new forum thread. As a result of the fork, it was delisted from Cryptsy between the 10th and 16th. On the 18th, Diamond was added to Coinmarketcap.com with an initial market cap of about $132,000. Diamond reached an all time high of about $436,159 in terms of market cap on the 29th. At this peak, one DMD was worth 0.00307995 BTC according to Cryptsy.

On the 10th of January 2014, the Facebook group was founded. On the 22nd, the Diamond Twitter page was founded. On the 27th, the Diamond forum went live (http://dmdcoin.net/forum/).

On the 19th of February, a wallet client (V 1.0.3) was released in order to fix connectivity in the network.

On the 1st of March, Diamond was added to www.coinpayments.net, a coin processing service.

On the 22nd of April, a third Bitcointalk thread was created. It was initiated by "popshot" to coincide with the move to the new Groestl algorithm (Diamond (DMD) Evolution v2.0). One day later, a client (V 1.0.4) was released. This update enabled future proof of stake.

On the 2nd of May, Diamond changed its mining algorithm from Scrypt to Groestl (more energy efficient, and also ASIC resistant). This began at block number 386,227. Also, the random lucky bonus blocks were removed. From this day, only solo mining was possible. It was not until August (~3 months) that mining pools were able to mine Diamond too.

On the 12th of June, "popshot" released a wallet client (V 2.0.2.1). This updated client made proof of stake function properly for the first time from coin number 450,000 (~26th of June).

On the 11th of July, a client (V 2.0.3) was released. It introduced "Coin Control" and "ToolTip Statistics".

On the 16th of September, problems with proof of work mining began. Proof of stake stabilised transactions, but at a slower rate. A new mandatory client (V 2.0.4) was released on the 22nd ready for proof of work reactivation on the 27th of September. Also in September, Diamond teamed up with Noblecoin in order to share resources and ideas.

www.facebook.com/dmdcoin
www.reddit.com/r/dmd
www.twitter.com/dmdcoin

MISCELLANEOUS

As the name suggests, Diamond is valuable, very difficult to mine and rare.

It was the first PoW/PoS hybrid coin to implement the random block feature from Luckycoin.

Diamond combines the best from Bitcoin/Litecoin/Novacoin/ Luckycoin/Florincoin. This provides excellent resistance to a 51% attack.

Its new developers describe Diamond as a ultra-scarce store of wealth with zero storage costs.

The whole design of diamond is to be a wealth storage coin aimed to be a good investment.

EXCHANGES

Coins-e (added on ~23/07/13)
Cryptsy (added on ~25/07/13)
AllCrypt (added on ~11/05/14)
useCryptos (added on ~17/08/14)

DMD TEAM

"JohnLuc" - Founder
Alex—Chief Executive Officier
Helmut—Chief Visionary Officier
Danbi—Lead Developer
Historical—Lead Web Developer

DMD

DIGIBYTE

"YOU STORE & SEND DATA IN MEGABYTES AND GIGABYTES, WHY NOT SEND MONEY IN DIGIBYTES?"

MultiAlgo Proof of Work

BLOCK REWARD DISTRIBUTION SCHEDULE TABLE

Block Phase	Block Number	Reward	Date of Initial Block
Pre-mine	1-1,439	72,000	~10th of January 2014
Pre-mine	1,440-1,526	16,000	~11th of January 2014
First Phase	1,527-5,759	16,000	~12th of January 2013
Second Phase	5,760-67,119	8,000	~14th of January 2014
1st 0.5% decrease	67,200-77,279	7,960	~28th of February 2014

The block reward continues to decrease by 0.5% every 10,080 blocks.

Block Phase	Block Number	Reward	Date of Initial Block
Last 0.5% decrease	399,840-399,999	6,746	~10th of December 2014
New Phase	400,000-	2,435	~10th of December 2014

The block reward continues to decrease by 1% every month.

DGB

DIGIBYTE

"YOU STORE & SEND DATA IN MEGABYTES AND GIGABYTES,
WHY NOT SEND MONEY IN DIGIBYTES?"

SPECIFICATION

Symbol:	DGB
Launched (Founder):	12th of January 2014 ("BitcoinTate" aka Jared Tate)
Hashing Algorithm:	MultiAlgo (SHa256, Scrypt, Skein, Qubit & Groestl)
Timestamping Algorithm:	Proof of Work
Address Begins With:	D
Maximum Coin Total:	21 billion
Block Time/Difficulty Retarget:	30 seconds/DigiShield
Coins per Block:	(see the first page)
Confirmations per Transaction:	Unknown
Pre-mine:	0.5% (105 million)

♦ Pre-mine generated from the blocks worth 72,000 as well as 87 blocks from the blocks worth 16,000.

♦ The block reward reduces by 0.5% approximately every week (every 7 days or 10,080 blocks) or halves approximately every two years.

♦ 52.5 million DGB for giveaways over first two months to encourage adoption of DGB. After the first 6 days of DigiByte's life over 44,105,165.259 million DigiBytes were dispersed from the giveaway account to merchants, developers, users and more in over 1,500 Transactions to DigiByte addresses.

♦ 52.5 million DGB for development expenses to further DigiByte and help it become a mainstream currency.

♦ Both the Giveaway and Development address are public in order to show transparency.

♦ 30 second blocks. Each block used to take 60 seconds.

♦ As of today, the pre-mine is zero. All coins pre-mined were donated or given away to users & charity.

♦ On the 10th of December, the block reward was reduced to 2,435 at block number 400,000. From this point, the block reward reduces by 1% each month.

http://digibyte.co   (Official Website)
http://explorer.cryptopoolmining.com/chain/DigiByte   (Block Explorer)
http://digibytetalk.com/   (Official Forum)   **DGB**

HISTORY

"YOU STORE & SEND DATA IN MEGABYTES AND GIGABYTES, WHY NOT SEND MONEY IN DIGIBYTES?"

User "DigiByte" announced the coin on Bitcointalk on the 10th of January 2014. Its launch was announced more than three days in advance with the aid of a countdown timer. In January, they welcomed "xploited" to the core development team. "xploited" was invaluable at getting a Android wallet up and running very quickly. On the 22nd of January, the DGB Android wallet was released. It was made available via the official website, not on Google Play.

Digibyte reached an all time high of about $641,004 in terms of market cap on the 6th of February 2014. This high coincided with its debut on Coined Up and Coinmarketcap.com. At this peak, it was worth 0.1 mBTC according to Coined Up.

On the 23rd of February, an update to the client source code was released in order to change the difficulty retarget and block reward reduction algorithms. The reward of the blocks would decrease by 0.5% each week, instead of halving every two years. The update was given the name "DigiByte v 2.0.0-DigiShield. A lot of testing was done over several days in order to be sure of its success. This was a mandatory update which users and pools had to install on or before the 28th of February (introduction of a hard fork). This change occurred as a result of the problems of high difficulty swings on multi-pool sites.

On the 8th of March, "DigiByte" posted a "DigiRoadMap" which details the future potential phases of the coin's development. On the 28th, a Windows wallet client (V 2.9) was released.

On the 9th of April, Jared Tate gave a speech at the New York Cryptocurrency Convention. One day later, the MAC OS X wallet (V 2.0.0) was released. It fixed the OpenSSL Heartbleed Bug. On the 30th, the Windows wallet client (V 2.9.1) was released. It implemented the latest Bitcoin protocol code. Also, the DigiByte Beginner guide video series was launched.

On the 2nd of May, Digibyte was mentioned by Brian Kelly live on CNBC's Fast Money programme. On the 14th, the Mac OS X wallet (V 2.9.1) become available for download after many days of development.

On the 16th of August, the MultiAlgo wallet client (V 3.0.1) was released. It had to be downloaded and installed before the fork at block 145,000.

On the 1st of September, DGB changed its mining algorithm from Scrypt to MultiAlgo (SHa256, Scrypt, Skein, Qubit & Groestl). It was the first altcoin to successfully fork to a multi algorithm state. This occurred at block number 145,000. On the 19th, Digibyte attended the Bitcoin Expo in Shanghai, China.

On the 27th of November, a wallet client (V 3.0.3) was released. It was a mandatory upgrade and introduced a hard fork. About two days later, Digibyte received a $250,000 Investment. It opened two new offices called DigiPay LLC of Santa Monica, California and DigiTrade International Limited of Hong Kong.

On the 10th of December, a hard fork occurred at block number 400,000. This reduced the block reward from 6,746 to 2,435 . A client (V 3.0.3) was released for users to install before this happened.

www.facebook.com/DigiByteCoin
www.reddit.com/r/Digibyte/
www.twitter.com/DigiByteCoin

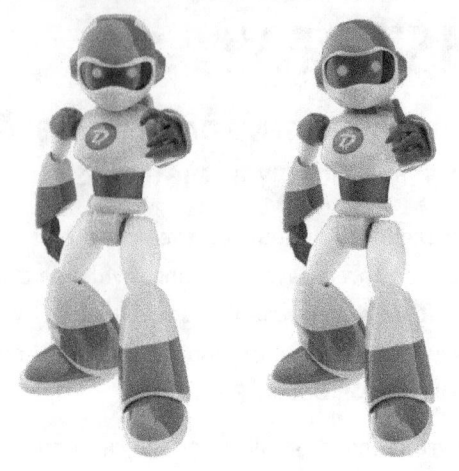

DigiMan design thanks to "bman3"

MISCELLANEOUS

Digibyte has its very own mascot called Digiman, a robot displaying the coin's logo.

The publicly posted pre-mine of DGB was used specifically in order to help its development and also to aid giveaways.

The developers are confident that the maximum potential coin total is adequate in order to avoid hoarding and not too high so as too dilute its value.

A quote from the developers is "DigiByte is Blazing fast! Much faster than Bitcoin & Litecoin, fast enough to buy coffee at Starbucks in a few seconds!"

"jdebunt" wrote frequent sections on DGB on www.cryptoarticles.com.

It was the first coin to fork to multi-algorithm mining.

EXCHANGES

Cryptokopen (added on ~17/01/14)
Coinmarket (added on ~19/01/14)
Cryptorush (added on ~29/01/14)
Coined UP (added on ~06/02/14)
MintPal (added on ~12/02/14)
OpenEx (added on ~18/02/14)
Comkort (added on ~03/03/14)
AllCrypt (added on ~04/03/14)
AGX (added on ~11/03/14)
Cryptsy (added on ~14/03/14)
Swissex (added on ~14/03/14)
Cryptokk (added on ~20/03/14)
Prelude (added on ~22/03/14)
Europex (added on ~07/04/14)
CryptoCzar (added on ~15/04/14)
Bittrex (added on ~20/08/14)
CEX.IO (added on ~28/09/14)

DGB TEAM

BitcoinTate—Founder, DigiByte.co Website, servers
xploited—Android wallet & source code, servers
Sifu - Project/training management & quality control.
Giggler - Alt-coin expert, IT support.
EDOG - Legal & editor.
Finchster - Expert programmer consultant.

bman3 - 3d promo graphics and promo video.
Instacash - Mac OSX wallet.
creativecuriosity - Public relations, quality control
Ice_Blade - IRC support, DigiBot developer.
WutriCoin - DigiByteTalk forum operator.
Cryos75 - Reddit tip-bot developer.

DGB

DIGITALCOIN

"A CURRENCY FOR THE DIGITAL AGE"

MultiAlgo Proof of Work

BLOCK REWARD DISTRIBUTION SCHEDULE TABLE

Block Phase	Block Number	Reward	Date of Initial Block
Initial Phase	1-523,799	20	~20th of May 2013
Second Phase	523,800-1,027,999	15	~5th of November 2013
Third Phase	1,028,000————-	5	~9th of December 2014

The block reward is indefinitely fixed at 5. This reduction to 5 DGC per block coincided with the change of hashing algorithm to Multi-Algo (Scrypt, SHA256, X11).

DGC

DIGITALCOIN

"A CURRENCY FOR THE DIGITAL AGE"
"AN ANONYMOUS, INSTANT, AND SECURE DIGITAL CURRENCY"

SPECIFICATION

Symbol:	DGC
Launched (Founder):	20th of May 2013 ("baritus")
Hashing Algorithm:	Multi-Algo (Scrypt, SHA256, X11)
Timestamping Algorithm:	Proof of Work
Address Begins With:	D
Total Coins:	48,166,000
Block Time/Difficulty Retarget:	20 seconds/108 blocks (~72mins)
Coins per Block:	(see the first page)
Confirmations per Transaction:	4
Pre-mine:	None

- The difficulty re-targeting time used to be every 1,080 blocks at 6 hours @ 20 seconds per block.

- Difficulty started at 0.00024414 with 6-8 retargets until desired difficulty of 1.

- Confirmations come in at an average of every 40 seconds.

- Rewards started at 20 and have since gone down to 5.

- Transactions are sent instantly and are confirmed in less than a minute.

- New total coins changed from ~144,500,000 to ~ 48,166,000. This began at block number 1,028,000.

- The hashing algorithm changed from solely Scrypt to Multi-Algo (Scrypt, SHA256 and X11) at block 1,028,000.

http://digitalcoin.co/en/   (Official Website)
https://dgc.blockr.io/   (Block Explorer)
http://digitalcoin.co/forums/   (Official Forum)
http://digitalcoin.foundation/   (Digitalcoin Foundation)

DGC

HISTORY

"A CURRENCY FOR A DIGITAL AGE"

"AN ANONYMOUS, INSTANT, AND SECURE DIGITAL CURRENCY"

On the 18th of May 2013, "baritus" announced Digitalcoin on a thread on Bitcointalk. Five days later, the official forum was launched (www.digitalcoin.co/forum). On the 26th, an updated client became available to download. It included updated checkpoints. On the 9th of June, Digitalcoin was added to the site Coinmarketcap.com. On the 1st of July, the official Facebook group of Digitalcoin was founded.

On the 21st of September, Cryptsy introduced the trading pair DGC/LTC.

On the 13th of October, "baritus" announced the introduction of a hard fork at block number 523,800 (reached on the 5th of November) This was a mandatory update (V1) which set the difficulty retarget to every 108 blocks instead of every 1,080 blocks. It also added a new checkpoint to the network. The block reward also changed from 20 to 15 coins at this same block number.

On the 2nd of November, the Digitalcoin Wallet Android App was released on Google Play.

On the 4th of December, Digitalcoin got mentioned in the "The Wall Street Journal" and "Yahoo Finance". It headlined Digitalcoin as possessing transaction speeds five times faster than Bitcoin. Digitalcoin reached an all time high of about $9,009,788 in terms of market cap on the 14th. At this peak, one DGC was worth 0.13 LTC according to Cryptsy. On the 19th, a new Windows client (V1.1 Mandatory) was released for download, followed by the Mac download three days later. This new client took effect at block number 625,800.

In January 2014, the design of the official website was updated. At the end of January, "followthecoin" spoke to "baritus" about the coin's progress as well as Securecoin, Argentum and the platform CryptoAve.

On the 21st of February, the exchange platform called CryptoAve went live. "baritus" had to apply a fix as regards BTC, SRC, ARG, PPC and LTC processing before the launch (CryptoAve closed on the 15th of Sept)

On the first day of March, the new Digitalcoin logo was chosen. One day later, the Digitalcoin Foundation Website (www.dgcfoundation.com/) was launched thanks to "Rawdog"

On the 9th of April, "Andrew Davidson" (DGC Project) gave a speech at the First Cryptocurrency Convention.

On the 8th of June, DGC 2.0 Core was released. The upgrade was not mandatory. It made the network more secure. On the 16th, the Facebook Multi-tipping App added Digitalcoin to their site.

In September, "baritus" stepped down from the lead development role. He handed over responsibility to the Digitalcoin Foundation, but said he will still remain part of the community. He will continue to host the website and forums. On the 17th, a new Bitcointalk thread was created by "kenel".

On the 27th of October, it was announced that Digitalcoin V3.0 was being fully tested and was scheduled to be ready by the end of November 2014. A change of the hashing algorithm from Scrypt to Multi-Algo was planned. Users were given several weeks notice before the change took place.

On the 3rd of December, a mandatory client (V 3.0) was released. A hard fork at block number 1,028,000 reduced the block reward to 5 DGC per block.

www.facebook.com/DigitalCoinDGC
www.reddit.com/r/digitalcoin
www.twitter.com/DigitalcoinDGC

An Anonymous, Instant, and Secure Digital Currency

MISCELLANEOUS

Its developers describe Digitalcoin as a coin that does not experience as much volatility as other cryptocurrencies do, so it tends to sustain its value better. This regard for stability is inherent in the design of Digitalcoin.

The "Digitalcoin Foundation" exists in order to protect, promote and implement projects which help long-term adoption of Digitalcoin. The official Digitalcoin website can be read in a vast number of different languages.

The creator of Digitalcoin is also behind two other altcoins, Securecoin and Argentum.

CryptoAve ceased to operate as an exchange on the 15th of September.

EXCHANGES

Crypto-Trade (added on ~07/05/13)
Cryptsy (added on ~22/05/13)
BTC38 (added on ~15/12/13)
Vircurex (added on ~17/12/13)
Bter (added on ~22/12/13)
Bitchanger (added on ~10/02/14)
Cryptorush (added on ~10/02/14)
CryptoAve (added on ~21/02/14)
C-Cex (added on ~14/03/14)
Prelude (added on ~21/03/14)
Cryptoczar (added on ~29/03/14)
Vault of Satoshi (added on ~10/04/14)
Swisscex (added on ~27/07/14)
Bittrex (added on ~19/09/14)

DGC FOUNDATION TEAM

kenel - President
Tsquared - Vice President
techbytes - Treasurer
butz - PR
RunningmanZ - PR

xawksow - Developer
CoHe - Designer
Rawdawg - Founding Member
samson - Developer
ahmed_bodi - Developer

DGC

DOGECOIN

"MUCH COIN, SO CRYPTO, WOW, SUCH CURRENCY"

Scrypt Proof of Work

BLOCK REWARD DISTRIBUTION SCHEDULE TABLE

Block Phase	Block Number	Reward	Date of Initial Block
Initial Phase	1-99,999	0-1,000,000 (random)	~8th of December 2013
1st Halving	100,000-144,999	0-500,000 (random)	~14th of February 2014
2nd Halving	145,000-199,999	250,000	~17th of March 2014
3rd Halving	200,000-299,999	125,000	~28th of April 2014
4th Halving	300,000-399,999	62,500	~15th of July 2014
5th Halving	400,000-499,999	31,250	~2nd of October 2014
6th Halving	500,000-599,999	15,625	~14th of December 2014
Fixed Phase	600,000+	10,000	~21st of February 2015

After an expected 98,437,500,000 coin supply, about 5.256 billion coins are mined per year from block 600,000. This is approximately a 5.34% inflation in the first year from about the 21st of February 2015.

DOGE

DOGECOIN

"FAVORED BY SHIBA INUS WORLDWIDE"
"MUCH COIN, SO CRYPTO, WOW, SUCH CURRENCY"

SPECIFICATION

Symbol:	DOGE, Đ
Launched (Founders):	8th of December 2013 (Jack Palmer & Billy Markus)
Hashing Algorithm:	Scrypt
Timestamping Algorithm:	Proof of Work
Address Begins With:	D
Total Coins:	(see the first page)
Block Time/Difficulty Retarget:	60 seconds/DigiSheid
Coins per Block:	(see the first page)
Confirmations per Transaction:	6
Pre-mine:	None

♦ It was based initially on Luckycoin (random block rewards). On the 17th of March, randomised block rewards were replaced by fixed block rewards.

♦ There was an initial coin cap of 100 billion coins, but this was changed. Now there is a built in inflation.

♦ Difficulty re-targeting used to be every 240 blocks (~4 hours) until the implementation of"Digishield" from Digibyte on the 17th of March 2014.

♦ Beginning at block number 600,000 there will be 5.2 billion coins released per year.

♦ Each block rewarded miners with a random number of coins before block 145,000.

♦ From block 371,337 the Dogecoin network began to accept Aux Proof of Work blocks from miners of other chains.

http://dogecoin.com/	(Official Website)
http://dogechain.info/chain/Dogecoin	(Block Explorer)
http://discuss.dogecoin.com/	(Official Forums)
http:/foundation.dogecoin.com/	(Dogecoin Foundation)

DOGE

HISTORY

"FAVORED BY SHIBA INUS WORLDWIDE"

"MUCH COIN, SO CRYPTO, WOW, SUCH CURRENCY"

DOGE

The idea of DOGE was first created by Billy Markus, a programmer from Portland, Oregon. A member of the Adobe Systems' Marketing Department called Jack Palmer arrived later on the scene. Jack purchased the internet domain (www.dogecoin.com). After discussions between these two individuals, work started on developing DOGE.

On the 8th of December 2013, the main DOGE thread on Bitcointalk was created by user "Dogecoin" and the Twitter page was created. Dogecoin was initially listed on Coined Up as DOGE/BTC on the 12th. On the 15th, Dogecoin was added to the site Coinmarketcap.com. On the 29th, the DOGE Facebook group was founded.

On 8th of January 2014, AltQuick.co was the first exchange to launch the trading pair DOGE/USD . Also in January, the Dogecoin community and foundation had a fundraiser in order to help send the Jamaican bobsled team to the Sochi Olympic Games. More than $30,000 worth of Dogecoin was raised. This fundraising campaign helped to increase the value of Dogecoin by about 50% in the space of 12 hours.

There was some controversy over whether or not the number of coins should be capped. On the 2nd of February, Jack Palmer said that there will be no cap. Dogecoin reached an all time high of about $93,698,583 in terms of market cap on the 12th of February. At this peak, it was worth 0.00295 mBTC according to Bter. On the same day, it reached 3rd place in terms of market cap on Coinmarketcap by surpassing Peercoin.

On the 12th of March, a client (V 1.6) was released. This had to be downloaded and installed before the 17th in time for a hard fork in the blockchain. It introduced fixed block rewards from block number 145,000 as well as the change of the difficulty re-targeting algorithm from every 240 blocks to "Digishield". On the 22nd, a campaign to raise a total of 40,000,000 ($30,000 at the time) Dogecoin to build a well in the Tana river basin in Kenya succeeded. This was in cooperation with charity: water.

On the 1st of April, Dogecoin was added to the international payments platform called GoCoin. On the 25th, the first Dogecoin Conference (Dogecon) was held in San Francisco.

On the 4th of May, Dogecoin helped to sponsor Josh Wise (Car number 98) to drive the Dogecar at Talladega, Alabama, USA. Commentators covering the Nascar event mentioned Dogecoin live on television. The first issue of the Dogecoin Magazine called "Very Much Wow" was released in May.

On the 19th of June, a client (V 1.7) was released. It moved Dogecoin to the Bitcoin 0.9 codebase.

On the 4th of August, it was announced that the Dogecoin blockchain would be enabled to accept auxiliary proof of work from other Scrypt chains. On the 24th, a client (V 1.8) was released. Users had to update to this client before block 371,337.

On the 11th of September, the hard fork that enables AuxPoW kicked in at block 371,337. Dogecoin merged mining with Litecoin began.

On the 6th of December, a party to celebrate one year of Dogecoin (Dogeversary) took place. Dogecoin founders Billy Markus and Jackson Palmer were present.

www.facebook.com/OfficialDogecoin
www.reddit.com/r/dogecoin/
www.twitter.com/dogecoin

MISCELLANEOUS

It was initially launched as a laugh but now has become one of the most established coins in a relatively short period of time.

Its success is most undoubtedly based on it being the first meme based coin. Shiba Inu from the "Doge meme".

Music videos on YouTube are a tribute to its early rise.

It is commonly used as a social tipping coin for users who create or post interesting content online.

A koinu is the smallest unit of DOGE valued at $1/10^8$ DOGE.

When you upvote a post or comment on the Dogecoin section of Reddit, a little rocket blasts off.

EXCHANGES

Coined Up (added on ~12/12/13)
Cryptsy (added on ~18/12/13)
Coins-e (added on ~19/12/13)
Vircurex (added on ~20/12/13)
CoinEX (added on ~12/01/14)
C-Cex (added on ~16/01/14)
Bter (added on ~18/01/14)
Poloniex (added on ~24/01/14)
Vault of Satoshi (added on ~29/01/14)
Swisscex (added on ~09/02/14)
AllCrypt (added on ~10/02/14)
Bittrex (added on ~13/02/14)
BTC38 (added on ~18/02/14)
MintPal (added on ~19/02/14)
Kraken (added on ~20/02/14)
Bleutrade (added on ~09/04/14)

DOGE TEAM

Billy Markus—Co-founder
Jack Palmer—Co-founder

DOGE

FASTCOIN

"SPEED IS JUST THE BEGINNING..."

Scrypt Proof of Work

BLOCK REWARD DISTRIBUTION SCHEDULE TABLE

Block Phase	Block Number	Reward	Date of Initial Block
Initial Phase	1-2,591,999	0-32	~29th of May 2013
1st Halving	2,592,000-5,183,999	0-16	~6th of June 2014
2nd Halving	5,184,000-7,775,999	0-8	~1st of June 2015
3rd Halving	7,776,000-10,367,999	0-4	~26th of May 2016
4th Halving	10,368,000-12,959,999	0-2	~21st of May 2017
5th Halving	12,960,000-15,551,999	0-1	~16th of May 2018
6th Halving	15,552,000-18,143,999	0>1	~11th of May 2019

The block reward (random) halves every ~360 days

FST

FASTCOIN

"SPEED IS JUST THE BEGINNING..."

SPECIFICATION

Symbol:	FST
Launched (Founder):	29th of May 2013 02:53 AM EST ("fast-coin")
Hashing Algorithm:	Scrypt
Timestamping Algorithm:	Proof of Work
Address Begins With:	f or g
Total Coins:	165,888,000
Block Time/Difficulty Retarget:	12 seconds/every hour
Coins per Block:	(see first page)
Confirmations per Transaction:	4
Pre-mine:	None

- FastCoin (FST) is the one of the fastest coins so far on the market. Fastcoin is a clone of Litecoin.

- Block rewards are randomised.

- 4 confirms per transaction. So every transaction will be confirmed in 48 seconds.

- Difficulty retargets every hour. It used accelerated retargets at the beginning (similar algorithm as that in Luckycoin).

- The coin reward to miners was an average of 16 coins per block initially. This halves every ~360 days (2,592,000 blocks).

http://fastcoin.ca/	(Official Site)
http://fst.webboise.com/chain/Fastcoin	(Block Explorer)
http://www.fastcointalk.org/	(Official Forum)

FST

HISTORY

"SPEED IS JUST THE BEGINNING..."

On the 29th of May 2013, "fast-coin" announced the coin on Bitcointalk. There was a lot of unfounded criticism on the forum regarding the very short block time of 12 seconds.

At the beginning of June, members of the Bitcointalk forum were happy of how easy solo mining the coin was. On the 21st of June, the first block explorer for FST was created thanks to "diatonic".

On the 6th of July, the Facebook group was founded. Besides this, the official website (www.fastcoin.ca) and the Twitter page were created. Four days later, updates to the GitHub source code and Windows client were made. Checkpoints were added and the Litecoin alert message was disabled. It was not mandatory, but recommended. On the 22nd of July, "fast-coin" announced that he was handing over responsibility of the coin to "Cheetahx". User "fast-coin" said he will still help out on the technical side of FST.

On the 31st of October, the current FST logo was chosen via community voting. The design of the logo was thanks to "Ohiwastedmylif ".

On the 18th of November, new Windows, Mac and Android wallet clients were released thanks to "Jase". "Jase" released the FST 8.5.1 client wallets on the 28th of November.

Fastcoin reached an all time high of about $2,810,288 in terms of market cap on the 1st of December 2013. At this peak, one FST was worth 0.05598 mBTC. It was only on Cryptsy at this time. On the 12th, the Fastcoin forum was launched (www.fastcointalk.org). Since the 19th it can be traded with LTC on Cryptsy.

On the 4th of January 2014, a new wallet client was released (V 0.8.5.3, 4th generation). It added checkpoints and disabled the Litecoin alert message feature. On the 8th, a video was published on YouTube titled "Why Fastcoin FST?".

On the 18th of February, an online merchant called Finite By Design started to sell Fastcoin Crypto Cards.

On the 1st of September, a client (V 0.8.7.2) was released.

www.facebook.com/FastCoin.ca
www.reddit.com/r/Fastcoin
www.twitter.com/fast_coin

MISCELLANEOUS

It has been designed to be the fastest form of cryptocurrency, hence the prefix "fast" before coin.

Fast transaction times are described by the developers as more suitable in retail as one won't need to wait long at the checkout before the first confirmation.

Fastcoin is used as a means to donate money to the "Farm to Family Food Project" based in the USA.

A coin called Flashcoin, with its 6 second block time, unseated Fastcoin as the fastest coin.

Fastcoin has one of the longest blockchains of all cryptocurrencies.

EXCHANGES

Cryptsy (added on ~06/06/13)
CoinEX (added on ~31/07/13)
Cryptorush (added on ~25/01/14)
CoinAccel (added on ~16/04/14)
Comkort (added on ~16/10/14)

FST TEAM

"fast-coin" - Founder
"Cheetahx" - Lead Developer

FST

FEATHERCOIN

"AN OPEN SOURCE INTERNET CURRENCY"

NeoScrypt Proof of Work

BLOCK REWARD DISTRIBUTION SCHEDULE TABLE

Block Phase	Block Number	Reward	Date of Initial Block
Initial Phase	1-204,638	200	~16th of April 2013
Second Phase	204,639-431,999	80	~25th of April 2014
NeoScrypt Began	432,000-839,999	80	~26th of October 2014
1st Halving	840,000-1,679,999	40	~5th of August 2015
2nd Halving	1,680,000-2,519,999	20	~10th of March 2017
3rd Halving	2,520,000-3,359,999	10	~14th of October 2018
4th Halving	3,360,000-4,199,999	5	~20th of May 2020
5th Halving	4,200,000-5,039,999	2.5	~24th of December 2021

And so on...

FTC

FEATHERCOIN

"AN OPEN SOURCE INTERNET CURRENCY"

SPECIFICATION

Symbol:	FTC (was originally FC)
Launched (Founder):	16th of April 2013 (Peter Bushnell)
Hashing Algorithm:	NeoScrypt
Timestamping Algorithm:	Proof of Work
Address Begins With:	6
Total Coins:	336 million
Block Time/Difficulty Retarget:	1 minute/every block
Initial Coins per Block:	(see the first page)
Confirmations per Transaction:	5
Pre-mine:	None

- Difficulty re-targeting used to be every 126 blocks with 504 block sampling and .25 damping.

- Difficulty retargets at every block now.

- Block reward halves every ~583 days from block number 840,000.

- The block time was 2.5 minutes, but is now 1 minute.

- Automatic check pointing to prevent 51% attacks

https://feathercoin.com/   (Official Website)
http://explorer.feathercoin.com/ (Block Explorer)
https://forum.feathercoin.com/   (Official Forum)

FTC

HISTORY

"AN OPEN SOURCE INTERNET CURRENCY"

Peter Bushnell announced the launch of Feathercoin on Bitcointalk on the 16th of April 2013. He had worked for about ten years as the head of ICT at Oxford University's Brasenose College beforehand. One day later, the first Feathercoin block explorer (http://explorer.feathercoin.cc:2002/) was created thanks to "blastbob". On the 20th, the first MAC wallet client was released. On the 22nd, the Feathercoin forum (https://forum.feathercoin.com/) was founded. On the 24th, users on Bitcointalk began to propose designs for potential Feathercoin coin logos. One day later, Peter Bushnell chose one of the designs by "nprussell". This is the current Feathercoin logo. On the 28th, a decision was made that FTC is the Feathercoin symbol, not FC. The official website was originally designed thanks to "altmine2".

On the 1st of May, an article was written on CoinDesk titled "Feathercoin shows heavyweight potential" On the 9th, it was added to the site Coinmarketcap.com.

On the 24th of June, a new Facebook group (www.facebook.com/feathercoinftc) was created.

On the 20th of July, the first offline Feathercoin transaction occurred at The Oxford Blue Pub. On the 22nd, Feathercoin, Phoenixcoin and Worldcoin formed a partnership called UNOCS.

Feathercoin reached an all time high of about $34,925,678 in terms of market cap on the 30th of November 2013. At this peak, one FTC was worth 0.00128 BTC according to BTC-e.

On the 13th of December, the official Twitter page was created. On the 18th, a client (V 0.8.5) was released.

On the 25th of January 2014, there was a meet up at The Oxford Blue Pub. At this meeting, laser etched Feathercoins, limited edition and handmade, were displayed. They were designed by @Netnerd's.

On the 13th of February, the newly designed Feathercoin official website was launched. Five days later, the Feathercoin forum also got improved in terms of its design and layout.

On the 7th of March, Chris Ellis gave a speech about Feathercoin and Bitcoin at Hull City Council. Also in the month of May, discussions about changing the hashing algorithm to NeoScrypt began.

On the 14th of April, a wallet client (V 0.8.6.2) was released. This update resolved blockchain sync issues and introduced a future hard fork at block number 204,639. On the 26th, 8,407 FTC were donated to the charity called Prostate Cancer UK. Also on this day, a Feathercoin ATM was revealed at The Oxford Blue Pub.

On the 1st of July, the FTC/USD trading pair was added to the Cryptsy trading exchange.

On the 26th of July, the hashing algorithm called NeoScrypt was created. It is designed as an "ASIC-resistant" algorithm for GPU and CPU miners.

On the 13th of October, a wallet (V 0.8.7.0) was released. It needed to be installed before the hard fork at block number 432,000 ready for the update to NeoScrypt. In late October 2014, Feathercoin officially switched over to NeoScrypt, a new type of memory-intensive hashing algorithm that supporters say will protect the coin from the influence of ASIC miners.

www.facebook.com/feathercoinftc
www.reddit.com/r/feathercoin
www.twitter.com/feathercoin

MISCELLANEOUS

Feathercoin's main spokesperson, Chris Ellis, features on many YouTube videos such as "The Bitcoin Group".

Feathercoin was the original light version of Litecoin, making it as light as a feather.

The Feathercoin community held a raffle fundraiser to help raise Feathercoins for Prostate UK. The winner was announced at the 4th Oxford Blue meet-up on the 22nd of February 2014.

EXCHANGES

Cryptonite (added on ~27/04/13)
Bter (added on ~30/04/13)
Vircurex (added on ~01/05/13)
BTC-e (added on ~02/05/13)
Cryptsy (added on ~22/05/13)
Crypto Trade (added on ~27/05/13)
Coins-e (added on ~13/07/13)
mcxNOW (added on ~24/09/13)
Bittylicious (added on ~11/12/13)
CoinEX (added on ~10/01/14)
Atomic Trade (added on ~21/01/14)
Vault of Satoshi (added on ~01/02/14)
C-Cex (added on ~06/02/14)
Bittrex (added on ~28/02/14)
AllCrypt (added on ~21/04/14)

FTC TEAM

Peter Bushnell—Founder/Development
ghostlander—Development
Chris Ellis—Promotion/PR
Wrapper—Development/Analysis/Testing
Ruthie—Engagements

Calem—Project Management/Digital Media
iawgoM—Website Development/Digital Media
uncle_muddy—Development/Merchant Adoption
Wellenreiter—Technical Development
MrWyrm—Forum Moderator

FTC

TiPS (FEDORACOIN)

"TiP OF THE HAT TO YOU"

Scrypt Proof of Work

BLOCK REWARD DISTRIBUTION SCHEDULE TABLE

Block Phase	Block Number	Reward	Date of Initial Block
Pre-mine	1-3	0-5,000,000	~22nd of December 2013
Initial Phase	4-51,999	0-5,000,000	~22nd of December 2013
1st Halving	52,000-103,999	0-2,500,000	~10th of February 2014
2nd Halving	104,000-207,999	0-1,125,000	~18th of March 2014
3rd Halving	208,000-415,999	0-625,000	~30th of May 2014
4th Halving	416,000-831,999	0-312,500	~14th of March 2015
5th Halving	832,000-1,663,999	0-156,250	~28th of December 2015
Static Phase	1,664,000——-	50,000	~12th of October 2016

Each block from block number 1,664,000 has a reward of 50,000 TIPS. This continues indefinitely.

TIPS

TiPS (FEDORACOIN)

""TiP OF THE HAT TO YOU""

SPECIFICATION

Symbol:	TIPS
Launched (Founder):	22nd of December 2013 ("Invisibel")
Hashing Algorithm:	Scrypt
Timestamping Algorithm:	Proof of Work
Address Begins With:	E
Total Coins:	500 billion
Block Time/Difficulty Retarget:	60 seconds/every block with KGW
Coins per Block:	(see the first page)
Confirmations per Transaction:	Unknown
Pre-mine:	First 3 blocks as a test

♦ Block rewards are randomised.

♦ Fedoracoin was the first coin to create a "mixing service". It is an innovative feature that allows people to send coins via a trusted third party. It makes untraceable the source of the coin.

♦ At block 52,000, the difficulty retargeting algorithm changed on Kimoto's Gravity Well.

http://www.fedoraco.in/   (Official Website)
http://insight.fedoracha.in/   (Block Explorer)
https://pay.withfedoraco.in/   (Payment Gateway)   **TIPS**

HISTORY

"TiP OF THE HAT TO YOU"

On the 22nd of December 2013, "MystPhysX" announced TIPS on Bitcointalk despite "Invisibel" being the lead developer at the time. Shortly after launch, a wallet client was released thanks to both "Invisibel" and "tonokip". Also on this day, the number of coins in a user's wallet went up by a multiple of five. The initial code was based on DOGE (it was based on a 100 billion coin cap). On the 24th, version 0.43 of the wallet was released that had to be installed before block 2,500. It implemented the DOGE difficulty re-targeting algorithm. On the 29th, Coined up added the TIPS/LTC trading pair, deactivating TIPS/BTC. One day later, "Invisibel" created a new Bitcointalk thread. On the 31st , TIPS was added to Coinmarketcap.com.

From the 14th of January 2014, "Invisibel" went quiet on Bitcointalk due to being threatened from hackers to halt coin development. During the absence, "theking7426" and "Fozy" created another thread on the forum for the community to take over. Also on this day, the logo competition closed with "donatel99" the winner with 20/43 votes casted. On the 26th, "Invisibel" returned to the Bitcointalk forum. He was surprised to see the community still flourishing and was inspired. He released a new Windows client (V 0.50) which helped rectify wallet sync issues. TiPS reached an all time high of about $3,456,564 in terms of market on the same day. At this peak, one TIPS was worth 0.00175 mLTC according to Coined Up. On the 30th, another wallet update (V 0.55) was released, but this was not mandatory. It implemented a change from DOGE code to LTC code (0.6). On the 31st, a new block explorer (http://chain.fedoraco.in) was introduced.

On the 2nd of February, the first coin mixing feature for a coin was announced by "Invisibel". A useable test beta version got running in about six hours. On the 4th, a wallet update (V 0.56) was released ready to be installed before block 52,000. This implemented Kimoto's Gravity Well as the difficulty re-targeting algorithm. On the 18th, a wallet client (V 0.60) was released which implemented the coin mixing feature.

On the 2nd of March, the new shield TiPS coin logo was designed. On the 10th, the first standalone FedoraCoin ticker was released by "srs2xcvbnm". Another version 0.03 of the ticker was released three days later. On the 16th, "orangefrogger" joined the development team. On the 26th, the new subreddit (http://www.reddit.com/r/tipscoin) went live thanks to "Fayen". One day later, the new TIPS Twitter page was created. On the 28th, "Martin Roy" created the Facebook group for all TiPS enthusiasts. The new Bitcointalk thread was created on the last day of March by user "FedoraCoin".

On the 11th of April, the Twitter TiP bot went live. On the 23rd, the World of TiPS website was launched that allows users to buy/sell products using the coin. Its founder was "hercules1600".

On the 4th of May, the TiPS payment processor became available (https://pay.withfedoraco.in/). Also in May, four Gridseed miner giveaway contests were held. Winners of this competiton were "mroyusa" (Reddit), "CryptoEthan" (Twitter), "arrakian" (Reddit) and "stafaniebraun" (Reddit).

At the end of July, a document titled "TIPS Plan" was published. It set out potential future plans and proposed projects.

In August, an "All About TIPS" public folder was released to detail the coin's future.

www.facebook.com/groups/fedoracoin/
www.reddit.com/r/FedoraCoin/
www.twitter.com/TiPS_FedoraCoin

"Fayen" created logo on 19/02/14 with 3D artwork help from "srs2xcvbnm"

"nerd_name" logo artwork above

New logo from 26/01/14 by "donatel99"

MISCELLANEOUS

The founder wished to have a fun coin replacement for DOGE.

"This kind of exchange disgusts me, instead of letting altcoins be a free-for-all they're basically letting whichever altcoin has the most money win. IMO This goes against the whole point of altcoins. (Quote from "Invisibel")

The coin was first released after Dogecoin in reference to the Fedora Meme.

From the 7th to the 24th of January 2014, the value of the coin went from 4 latoshis to 40 latoshis. On the 24th of January, the volume of the preceding 24 hours was ~$170,000.

"icanprogram" took over lead development from "Invisibel".

EXCHANGES

Coined Up (added on ~27/12/13)
AllCoin (added on ~26/01/14)
Cryptsy (added on ~26/01/14)
Cryptorush (added on ~31/01/14)
OpenEx (added on ~20/02/14)
Bter (added on ~23/02/14)
Comkort (added on ~26/02/14)
NewAltEx (added on ~16/03/14)
Coin-Swap (added on ~28/03/14)
Europex (added on ~03/04/14)
Swisscex (added on ~15/05/14)

TIPS TEAM

invisibel - TiPS founder
icanprogram - TiPS lead developer
MystPhysX - Mac OS developer
Hercules1600 - World of TiPS founder
orangefrogger - Web designer

Fayens - Graphic designer, CSS pro
Cinnajerry - Reddit community manager
Fargusson - BitcoinTalk and French community manager
WigitGetIt - BitcoinTalk English community manager
DarkVenu - BitcoinTalk Italian community manager

TIPS

FRANKO

"FRANKO IS FREEDOM"

Scrypt Proof of Work

BLOCK REWARD DISTRIBUTION SCHEDULE TABLE

Block Phase	Block Number	Reward	Date of Initial Block
Initial Phase	1-22,471,625	0.25	~11th of May 2013
First Halving	22,471,626-44,943,251	0.125	~20th of September 2034
Second Halving	44,943,252-67,414,877	0.0625	~31st of January 2056
Third Halving	67,414,878-89,886,503	0.03125	~11th of June 2077
Fourth Halving	89,886,504-112,358,130	0.015625	~21st of October 2098

And so on...

FRK

FRANKO

"FRANKO IS FREEDOM"
"NON NOBIS SOLUM, SED OMNIBUS"

SPECIFICATION

Symbol:	FRK
Launched (Founder):	11th of May 2013 6:01 PM (UTC) (Christopher Franko)
Hashing Algorithm:	Scrypt
Timestamping Algorithm:	Proof of Work
Address Begins With:	F
Total Coins:	11,235,813
Block Time/Difficulty Re-target:	30 seconds/Kimoto's Gravity Well
Coins per Block:	(see the first page)
Confirmations per Transaction:	5
Pre-mine:	None

◆ Difficulty used to re-target every 720 blocks (~6 hours). It changed to KGW on the 26th of January 2014.

◆ Block reward halves every 22,471,626 blocks (~22 years). The first halving of the block reward will occur when roughly half the coins have been mined (~5,617,906 coins)

◆ Franko is based on the Litecoin protocol but differs from Litecoin in that it is 8x more rare and a lot faster.

http://frankos.org   (Official Website)
http://coinplorer.com/FRK   (Block Explorer)
http://forum.frankos.org/   (Official Forum)

FRK

HISTORY

"FRANKO IS FREEDOM"

"NON NOBIS SOLUM, SED OMNIBUS"

FRK

On the 11th of May 2013, user "defaced" announced the launch of FRK on Bitcointalk and the Facebook group was founded. Two days later, the first client update (V 0.6.3.1) was released. This update implemented new checkpoints as well as lowering minimum transaction fees. On the 21st of May, the client (V 0.6.3.2) was released. It was a mandatory requirement as it ensured users kept on the correct blockchain. A checkpoint was added at block number 27,650. On the 28th, client (V 0.6.3.3) was released as a fix to the block reward schedule that was initially set for the block reward to halve every 100,000 blocks. As a mandatory update, it changed the code so that the block reward will halve initially after half the total coins have been mined. Also on this day, Franko was listed on Cryptsy as the trading pair FRK/BTC.

On the 9th of June, Franko was added to the site Coinmarketcap.com.

On the 22nd of July, jaysjerky@live.com began accepting Franko for Jerkies.

Franko reached an all time high of about $1,116,754 in terms of market cap on the 30th of November 2013. At this peak, one FRK was worth 0.0141 BTC according to Cryptsy

On the 10th of December, Christopher Franko participated in the show called "Mad Bitcoins", a show that broadcasts on YouTube. On the 17th, the client (V 0.8.5.2) was released.

On the 18th of January 2014, a client (V 0.8.5.3) was released (mandatory) ready for the change of the difficulty re-targeting algorithm to KGW. This change occurred at block 400,000 on the 26th of January.

On the 5th of February, the trading pair FRK/USD became available on the exchange C-Cex. On the 26th, Christopher Frank was interviewed by Catherine Glover, the director of the "Washington Beaufort County Chamber of Commence". It was broadcasted in the first week of March on multiple local television channels.

On the 18th of March, the trading pair FRK/LTC was added to Cryptsy. On the 20th, Christopher Franko attended an event at the Yacht & County Club in Washington NC. He cut the ribbon at this event.

On the 8th of April, the client (V) was released for users to install before block number 646,120. This fixed an issue with KGW.

On the 16th of July, a fully functioning Franko ATM was revealed by Christopher Franko. It is based on Sky Hook's open source Bitcoin ATM.

On the 30th of October, an official document listing all the bounties for Franko was released. It lists certains projects for which potential developers can build for a given specified Franko reward.

On the 16th of December, the Franko to USD (FRK/USD) conversion rate was added to the official website.

www.facebook.com/Frankosorg?ref=br_tf
www.reddit.com/r/Franko/
www.twitter.com/FrankoCurrency

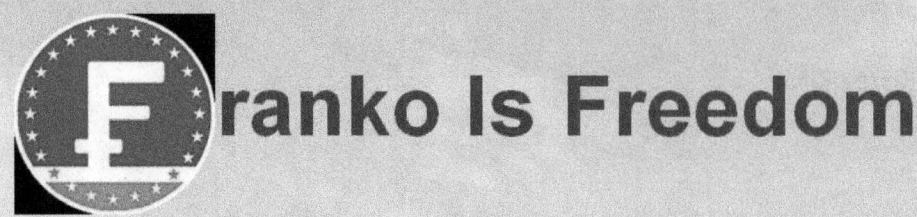

Franko Is Freedom

Non nobis solum, *Sed* omnibus.

Find Out More

MISCELLANEOUS

Non nobis solum, sed omnibus! It is a latin motto which means one should contribute to the general greater good of humanity, apart from their own interests.

A white paper written by the founder Christopher Franko is available to view from the official website. It is titled "Franko: A Distributed Autonomous Corporation Designed for the next 500 Years".

EXCHANGES

Cryptsy (added on ~28/05/13)
Coins-e (added on ~23/07/13)
Swisscex (added on ~05/02/14)
Pmtocoins (added on ~05/02/14)
C-Cex (added on ~05/02/14)
BTC CC (added on ~06/03/14)
Poloniex (added on ~16/03/14)
CoinAccel (added on ~16/04/14)
Cryptex (added on ~04/10/14)

FRK TEAM

Christopher Franko - Founder/Lead Developer

FRK

GOLDCOIN

"THE GOLD STANDARD OF CRYPTOCURRENCY"

Scrypt Proof of Work

BLOCK REWARD DISTRIBUTION SCHEDULE TABLE

Block Phase	Block Number	Reward	Date of Initial Block
Phase 1	1-200	10,000	~15th of May 2013
Phase 2	201-2,200	1,000	~15th of May 2013
Phase 3	2,201-44,999	500	~15th of May 2013
Phase 4	45,000-307,799	45	~2nd of August 2013
Phase 5	307,800-570,599	31.447	~2nd of August 2014
Phase 6	570,600-	24.038	~2nd of August 2015

There is a formula that calculates the coins per block (Block Reward) from the 2nd of August in a certain year. It is Block Reward = $50/\{1.1 + [0.49*(Year-2013)]\}$ (where the year is YYYY, not YY)

GLD

GOLDCOIN

"THE GOLD STANDARD OF CRYPTOCURRENCY"
"MAY ALL YOUR BITCOIN DREAMS TURN TO GOLD"

SPECIFICATION

Symbol:	GLD
Launched (Founder):	15th of May 2013 ("gldcoin")
Hashing Algorithm:	Scrypt
Timestamping Algorithm:	Proof of Work
Address Begins With:	D or E
Total Coins:	123,423,900
Block Time/Difficulty Retarget:	(see below)
Coins per Block:	(see the first page)
Confirmations per Transaction:	6
Pre-mine:	None

- The original total coin circulation cap was initially set at 100 million

- There was a 2.5 minute block time up to and including block 44,999.

- There was a difficulty retarget every 504 blocks up to and including block 44,999.

- From now on, the block time is 2 minutes.

- From now on, the difficulty retarget is every 60 blocks.

- A Unique and innovative 51% attack defence system (after block 100,000) protects the network by preventing hash power from being added too quickly. It basically gives more power to the little guy by removing the advantage of someone using an industrial strength mining rig jumping on the network for some quick and easy coins .

- Coin generation rules modelled after physical gold.

- Block reward finishes in 2113.

http://gldcoin.com/   (Official Website)
http://gld.cryptocoinexplorer.com/   (Block Explorer)
https://www.gldtalk.org/   (Official Forum)

GLD

HISTORY

"THE GOLD STANDARD OF CRYPTOCURRENCY"

"MAY ALL YOUR BITCOIN DREAMS TURN TO GOLD"

Goldcoin was announced on Bitcointalk on the 15th of May 2013 by "gldcoin". Two days later, www.gldcointalk.org was created thanks to "kr4x". On the 19th, "503guy" created the first GLD block explorer (http://gld.block-chain.net). Eight days after launch, GLD was added to Cryptsy on both the BTC and LTC markets. One week later, Cryptsy removed direct trading with BTC, which left just GLD/LTC trading.

On the 2nd of June, the first post was made by "MicroGuy" in the GLD Bitcointalk thread. "If anyone wants to give me a deal, I would like to buy some GLD for BTC :D" was posted by him. On the 5th, two forums were founded. "BitcoinBoard" founded the site www.gldcoinforum.com and "MicroGuy" founded the site www.gldtalk.org. Some controversy then began over having two forums. On the 6th, the Facebook group for the Goldcoin forum was founded. One day later, a campaign began to help strengthen the Goldcoin network through adding mining hashing power. This was named "The Miner Bonus Program". It paid miners $8 per day for every 1,000K Hashes of additional hashing power until the 17th of June. This initiative was a success after which the network returned to sustainable levels. On the 11th, "gldcoin" handed over responsibility of Goldcoin to "MicroGuy". The domain www.gldcoin.com was sold to "MicroGuy" for about 3 BTC. A new Bitcointalk thread was created by "MicroGuy" on the same day. On the 14th, it was added to Coinmarketcap.com. On the 25th, www.gldcoin.com went live. By the end of June, a solid and reliable development team lead by "akumabum" was in place.

On the 24th of August, the GLD/BTC market was re-introduced on Cryptsy. On the 31st, the GLD Android Wallet App was released. This was made available through the official website.

On the 11th of October, a client (V 0.7) was released (mandatory) before block 100,000. This introduced the new 51% defence system into the GLD network. On the 24th, the official Twitter page was created. On the same day, another GLD Bitcointalk thread was created. On the 31st, block 100,00 was reached.

On the 27th of November, a client (V 0.7.1.6) update was released. It was mandatory and had to be downloaded and installed before the blockchain forked at block number 117,000.

Goldcoin reached an all time high of about $4,854,312 in terms of market cap on the 1st December 2013. At this peak, one GLD was worth 0.00013995BTC.

On the 11th of January 2014, another goldcointalk Facebook group was created.

On the 9th of April 2014, the client of the GLD wallet was updated to fix the OpenSSL Heartbleed Bug.

On the 17th of June, a Goldcoin Talent Contest began. People had to make a video in which they promoted GLD and their particular talent. This ended on the 31st of July. The prize was 5,000 GLD or a $100 giftcard.

On the 9th of September, "kreno777" was the first person to win a GLD Giftcard.

On the 29th of November, an event called the South African Goldcoin Conference was held in Port Elizabeth thanks to South African businessman and investor, Jason Swart. They have also started negotiations to rent the venue again for the next Goldcoin conference in January 2015.

www.facebook.com/groups/goldcointalk/
www.reddit.com/r/goldcoin
www.twitter.com/GoldCoinInfo

User "1Peter"

OLD BLOCK SCHEDULE:
1 – 200 Blocks – 10000 GLD
201 – 2200 Blocks – 1000 GLD
2201 – 26200 Blocks – 500 GLD
26201 – 48700 Blocks – 400 GLD
48700 – 173700 Blocks – 200 GLD
173701 – 673700 Blocks – 100 GLD

MISCELLANEOUS

A name meaning "value" to billions of people worldwide.

Coin generation rules modelled after physical gold.

The new developers had to fix bugs in the code which otherwise would had permitted unlimited coin generation.

The community helped to improve the coin's logo so as to make it look more professional.

"MicroGuy" broadcasts regular videos called "The Goldcoin Report" on YouTube.

"MicroGuy" is the founder of the current Goldcoin Forum (https://www.gldtalk.org).

EXCHANGES

Cryptsy (added on ~23/05/13)
CoinEX (added on ~21/08/13)
Bittrex (added on ~28/03/14)

GLD TEAM

"akumabum" - Lead Developer
"MicroGuy" - PR Marketing

GLD

HOBONICKELS

"THE STREET'S CRYPTO-CURRENCY"

Scrypt Proof of Work/Proof of Stake

BLOCK REWARD DISTRIBUTION SCHEDULE TABLE

Block Phase	Block Number	Reward	Date of Initial Block
First Phase	1-99,999	5	~24th of July 2013
Second Phase	100,001-999,999	5	~27th of August 2013
Third Phase	1,000,000-	5	~4th of July 2014

The block reward of proof of work mining has always been 5 HBN.
Proof of stake minting has been possible since the 27th of April 2014.

HBN

HOBONICKELS

"THE STREET'S CRYPTO-CURRENCY"

SPECIFICATION

Symbol:	HBN
Launched (Founder):	24th of July 2013 ("Thundertoe")
Hashing Algorithm:	Scrypt
Timestamping Algorithm:	Hybrid Proof of Work/Proof of Stake
Address Begins With:	E or F
Total Coins:	120 million
Block Time/Difficulty Retarget:	30 seconds
Coins per Block:	5
Confirmations per Transaction:	25 for PoW/PoS blocks, 6 for regular transactions
Pre-mine:	None

- HBN was cloned and customised from the Novacoin source code by multiple developers.

- It was launched as a hybrid proof of work/proof of stake coin, and still is. Proof of stake was built into the code from day one, but has been active since the 27th of April 2014.

- HoboNickels features a generous super stake and one of the most advanced QT wallet clients available for any coin on the market, featuring Multi-Wallet Functionality, Advanced Coin Control, Stake for Charity and Faststaker.

- Proof of stake is 2% stake every 10 days, 100% yearly degrading over difficultly. This PoS percentage is designed to decrease within the range 2-5% as more people stake the coin (inflation control).

- The PoW block reward does not halve at any time. It has been 5 HBN per block since launch.

- It implements the secure feature of Automated Block Checkpoints.

- The plan is to move to a mostly proof of stake coin over the next few years.

http://hobonickels.info/   (Official Website)
http://hbn.blockx.info/   (Block Explorer)

HBN

HISTORY

"THE STREET'S CRYPTO-CURRENCY"

HBN

Hobonickels was announced on the Bitcointalk forum on the 24th of July 2013 by user/developer "thundertoe". "thundertoe" is quoted as saying that the idea of Hobonickels originated on the chatbox of Cryptsy. Members of this exchange decided to pay tribute to the hobo and devoted this coin to "cryptohobo" (a community user who was initially unaware). A team of developers ("thundertoe", "Tranz" and "mullick") initially worked on Hobonickels.

Hobonickels was initially listed on Cryptsy on the 4th of August 2013.

In September, the wallet client was updated to version 1.2 in order to correct the percentage of stake allowed. It was only issuing a stake of 0.2%, not the official 2%. It was "Tranz" who found this flaw in the code. He then became the leading developer of HBN.

In December, the wallet client was again updated to version 1.3.0.0 due to slow client loading times, crashes of encrypted wallet and troubles with the blockchain. Also, on the 20th of December, Hobonickels was added to the site Coinmarketcap.com.

On the 18th of January 2014, the Hobonickel Facebook group was founded.

Hobonickels reach an all time high of about $777,588 in terms of market cap on the 15th of February. At this peak, one HBN was worth 0.3989 mBTC.

On the 30th of March, "Tranz" announced that stake of charity testing was underway and would be implemented into a future wallet client.

On the 3rd of April, cryptofunds.pw allowed users to trade HBN with both BTC and LTC. On the 9th, "Tranz" released the Stake of Charity Wallet (V 1.4). On the 21st, the community announced a Hobonickels GPU contest. The prize was a XFX 7950 card hashing machine. Members had to guess the first seven successive numbers of the first proof of stake block hash which occurred six days later. On the 30th of April, HBN reached a new all time high of about $969,140 in terms of market cap. At this peak, one HBN was worth 0.788 mBTC according to Cryptsy.

On the 16th of May, a newly designed block explorer (http://hbn.blockx.info) was created thanks to "unick".

On the 10th of July, it was announced that work on client (V 1.5) had been started.

On the 1st of September, the first beta client (V 1.4.7.0) was ready. Four days later, the second beta client (V 1.4.8.0) was released. This new client corrected code from the previous beta release.

On the 17th of October, the final beta client (V 1.4.9.99) was released. Version 1.5 is expected to be released at the end of 2014.

www.facebook.com/pages/Hobonickels-HBN-Crypto-Currency/672818916094322
www.reddit.com/search?q=hobonickels

MISCELLANEOUS

"Digitalhobo" designed and carved the Hobonickel logo.

Hobonickels have been a historical pastime for over one hundred years. Digitalhobo continues this legacy of carving a Hobonickel into various forms of artwork.

HBN was the first coin to use Multi-Wallet functionality.

EXCHANGES

Cryptsy (added on ~04/08/13)
CoinEX (added on ~01/10/13)
Atomic Trade (added on ~21/01/14)
Cryptofunds (added on ~03/04/14)
Comkort (added on ~07/10/14)

HBN TEAM

"thundertoe" - Founder
"Tranz" - Lead Developer
"adria33" - Reddit Moderator

HBN

INFINITECOIN

"GET REAL MONEY WITH INFINITE POSSIBILITIES!"

Scrypt Proof of Work

BLOCK REWARD DISTRIBUTION SCHEDULE TABLE

Block Phase	Block Number	Reward	Date of Initial Block
Initial Phase	1-86,399	524,288	~5th of June 2013
1st Halving	86,400-172,799	262,144	~5th of July 2013
2nd Halving	172,800-259,199	131,072	~4th of August 2013
3rd Halving	259,200-345,599	65,536	~28th of September 2013
4th Halving	345,600-431,999	32,768	~27th of October 2013
———————	———————	———————-	———————————
16th Halving	1,382,400-1,468,799	8	~22nd of October 2014
17th Halving	1,468,800-1,555,199	4	~21st of November 2014
18th Halving	1,555,200-1,641,599	2	~21st of December 2014
19th Halving	1,164,600—————	1	~20th of January 2015

IFC

INFINITECOIN

"GET REAL MONEY WITH INFINITE POSSIBILITIES!"

SPECIFICATION

Symbol:	IFC
Launched (Founder):	5th of June 2013 ("fisheater")
Hashing Algorithm:	Scrypt
Timestamping Algorithm:	Proof of Work
Address Begins With:	i
Total Coins:	90.6 billion
Block Time/Difficulty Retarget:	30 seconds/every block
Coins per Block:	524,288 (2^19) (initially)
Confirmations per Transaction:	3
Pre-mine:	None

- Difficulty re-targeting used to occur every 120 blocks or approximately every hour before block number 248,000.

- The block reward halved every 86,400 blocks from an initial reward of 524,288 (2^19).

- It will have 1142.86 times as many coins as LTC, and the difficulty with which coins are produced is adjusted more frequently.

- Difficulty retargets every block, with accelerated retargets at the beginning.

- First working example of a network to be based mostly on transaction fees.

- Transaction fees are optional, but 1% is required on transactions with inputs greater than 10 IFCs.

- Advanced checkpointing limits the effect of 51% attacks.

http://www.infinitecoin.com   (Official Website)
http://exploretheblocks.com:2750/ (Block Explorer)
http://infinitecointalk.org   (Official Forum)

IFC

HISTORY

"GET REAL MONEY WITH INFINITE POSSIBILITIES!"

IFC

Infinitecoin was announced on Bitcointalk on the 5th of June 2013 by "fisheater". On the 24th, "heju22" suggested an improvement to the original Infinitecoin logo (gold/silver) without initial interest. However, after the design was published, the new logo was adopted. One day later, the wallet client was updated for the first time to version 1.1. On the 29th, the original official website was launched thanks to "nzdude" and "heju22". One day later, the current website (www.infinitecoin.org) was launched thanks to "heju22".

Version 1.2 of the wallet was released on the 4th of July in order to fix coin limits. It also introduced further checkpoints. On the 8th, the Infinitecoin Facebook group was founded. Two days later it was added to Coinmarketcap.com. On the 25th, Cryptsy closed down the IFC/BTC market and only the IFC/LTC trading pair remained. Version 1.3 of the wallet was released on the 31st to deal with minimum transaction fees.

On the 12th of August, Infinitecoin reached 15th position of total market capitalisations at a market cap of about $118,396 according to the website Coinmarketcap.com. On the 28th, a client (V 1.4) was released. It disabled transaction fees. Users had to upgrade before the 1st of September.

After many weeks of problems concerning the difficulty retargeting of Infinitecoin, version 1.8 of the wallet was released. This was a mandatory update. Users had to upgrade before a hard fork occurred at block number 248,000. Instead of Infinitecoin utilising the standard proof of work linear retarget formula every 120 blocks, the PPC retarget formula was implemented at each block from that block.

On the 25th of September, Cryptsy suspended IFC/LTC trading for four days. This was due to issues with the blockchain. On the 30th, the trading pair IFC/XPM opened on Cryptsy.

The total market capitalisation of Infinitecoin surpassed $1 million on the 26th of November. One day later, Cryptsy suspended trading of Infinitecoin for about one day due to a forked blockchain.

On the 4th of December, "fisheater" stepped down from heading the coin due to personal circumstances, but said he will still continue to support the coin. "Tecshare" took over and he appointed "uRndUsr" as the new lead developer. A new Bitcointalk thread was created by "Tecshare" on the 4th of December.

Infinitecoin reached an all time high of about $13,518,302 in terms of market cap on the 27th of January 2014. At this peak, one IFC was worth 0.00697 mLTC according to Bter.

On the 12th of February, the IFC/BTC trading pair was re-introduced on Cryptsy. Also in February, the Infinitecoin Android Wallet App was released on Google Play.

On the 9th of April, Loring Small, not the lead developer, gave a speech at the New York Cryptocurrency Convention. One day later, version 1.8.7 patched the wallet due to the Heartbleed Bug.

On the 2nd of July, a new Facebook group was created (https://www.facebook.com/IFCInfinitecoin).

On the 3rd of September, "Tecshare" assured the community that the Infinitecoin project had not been abandoned. On the 12th, a new Infinitecoin promotional video was put together and published on YouTube.

www.facebook.com/IFCInfinitecoin
www.reddit.com/r/infinitecoin/
www.twitter.com/Infinitecoin_US

MISCELLANEOUS

It is a clone of LiteCoin, but has many more coins.

The vast majority of Infinitecoin have now been mined. This means that the end of the block reward period is soon to be over and Infinitecoin will have to rely on the fact that fee's are included in the transactions.

IFC TEAM

"fisheater"—Founder
"Tecshare" - Community Manager
"uRndUsr" - Lead Developer

IFC

KITTEHCOIN

"THE PREMIERE PEER-TO-PEER INTERNET CURRENCY FOR CLASSY KITTEHS"

Scrypt Proof of Work

BLOCK REWARD DISTRIBUTION SCHEDULE TABLE

Block Phase	Block Number	Reward	Date of Initial Block
Initial Phase	1-200,000	1,000-50,000	~24th of December 2013
1st Halving	200,001-400,000	1,000-25,000	~8th of April 2014
2nd Halving	400,001-500,000	1,000-12,500	~14th of September 2014
3rd Halving	500,001-600,000	1,000-6,250	~22nd of November 2014
4th Halving	600,001-700,000	1,000-3,125	~30th of January 2015
Final Phase	700,001-	2,000 (flat)	~9th of April 2015

Once 25 billion coins has been reached, there will be a certain inflation per annum. This is based on the 2,000 coins mined per block beginning approximately on the 9th of April 2015.

MEOW

KITTEHCOIN

"THE PREMIERE PEER-TO-PEER INTERNET CURRENCY FOR CLASSY KITTEHS"

SPECIFICATION

Symbol:	MEOW
Launched (Founder):	24th of December 2013 ("lonestar108")
Hashing Algorithm:	Scrypt
Timestamping Algorithm:	Proof of Work
Address Begins With:	K
Total Coins:	25 billion
Block Time/Difficulty Retarget:	60 seconds/KGW
Coins per Block:	(see the first page)
Confirmations per Transaction:	Unknown
Pre-mine:	None

- A special rewards system exists. Block rewards are random with a minimum 1,000 MEOW per block. This ceases to be the case after block number 700,000.

- The difficulty used to re-target every hour until block 126,500.

- The block time used to be 30 seconds until block number 126,500.

- The total number of coins was set at 50 billion until block 126,500.

https://kittehcoin.info/   (Official Website)
http://kittehcoinblockexplorer.com/chain/Kittehcoin   (Block Explorer)
http://kittehcoin.info/forums/index.php   (Official Forum)

MEOW

HISTORY

"THE PREMIERE PEER-TO-PEER INTERNET CURRENCY FOR CLASSY KITTEHS"

"lonestar108" announced the launch of Kittehcoin on Bitcointalk on the 24th of December 2013. One day later, the first block explorer (http://kitexplorer.tk) was created thanks to "nocoin". On the 29th, the first Twitter page was created (www.twitter.com/KittehCoinTeam).

Kittehcoin was initially listed on Coined Up as the trading pair MEOW/BTC. Coined Up then introduced the trading pairs MEOW/LTC and MEOW/DOGE to their exchange later on. On the 4th of January 2014, the official forum (http://forums.kittehcoin.info) was launched thanks to "danosphere". One day later, "Ng93" officially became a member of the development team. On the 6th, "lonestar108" announced that he could no longer be the lead developer of the coin, but said he would continue to contribute to the future of Kittehcoin. Instead, "danosphere" became the lead developer. On the 12th, the Kittehcoin Facebook group was founded. One day later, the current Kittehcoin coin logo was chosen via a community vote. It was designed by "sebastien1234". On the 24th, Kittehcoin was added to Coinmarketcap.com. Kittehcoin reached an all time high of about $3,840,475 in terms of market cap on the 27th of January. At this peak, one MEOW was worth 0.00089 mBTC.

On the 4th of February, the coin was re-launched with a new coin specification and a new wallet client (V 0.6.4.1) was released. A new Bitcointalk thread was created by "danosphere" in order to mark this occasion. Also on this day, the current Twitter page was created. Another client (V 0.8.6.2) was released on the 14th which had to be installed before block 126,500. It incorporated code for the switch to the Kimoto Gravity Well Difficulty Re-target Algorithm. In addition to this, the total coin cap halved to 25 billion and the block time doubled to 60 seconds. This change took effect at block number 126,250 on the 15th of February.

On the 9th of March, altoutlet.com added Kittehcoin and so began to accept MEOW as a form of payment for merchandise. Two days later, a leadership board called "KittehCommand" was formed by "danosphere", "jonn4y", "Mortimer452" and "sebastien1234". On the 15th, Kittehcoin was added to the merchant processing platform called Moolah.

On the 16th of April, "danosphere" announced a future hard fork in the blockchain. He also said that he planned to vacate the lead development role. His reasons for wanting to step down were due to personal commitments. He wanted to leave the coin in capable hands.

In May, "TheMightyX" co-ordinated with "danosphere" to step in and take over Kittehcoin management.

For a few months, much discussion about the future of Kittehcoin occurred. The topics most discussed were about possible proof of stake implementation, KGW fixes and changes to the block reward schedule. "danosphere" assured the Kittehcoin community that a team is working hard to revive the coin.

In early July, Cryptsy removed the MEOW/BTC trading pair from their exchange. This was most likely due to the very small value of one MEOW in comparison to that of one single Bitcoin. MEOW/LTC remained.

Kittehcoin is now undergoing a revival by a small team including a user called "rodux".

www.facebook.com/kittehcoin
www.reddit.com/r/KittehCoin
www.twitter.com/Kittehcoin

MISCELLANEOUS

The developers thought it was listed on an exchange a little prematurely, before the community was really ready for it.

"danosphere" and eleven others stepped up to the plate in an unprecedented effort to take over and improve a coin after "lonestar108" stepped down from the lead development role.

EXCHANGES

Coined Up (added on ~03/01/14)
Coin-Swap (added on ~29/01/14)
Cryptsy (added on ~04/02/14)
Poloniex (added on ~04/02/14)
NewAltEx (added on ~08/02/14)
Cryptorush (added on ~16/02/14)
Comkort (added on ~20/02/14)
Bittrex (added on ~28/02/14)
Prelude (added on ~17/03/14)
AllCrypt (added on ~25/03/14)
Europex (added on ~26/04/14)
C-Cex (added on ~06/06/14)

MEOW TEAM

augi - OSX and linux wallet dev
AustinDizzy - Subreddit Mod
coderboo - Crypto Expert
danosphere - Lead dev, jack of all trades
jonn4y - Web dev, iOS Dev, ninja
Kotina - Web dev, master css and bootstrapper
lmfsthefounder - Android Dev, service developer

majsta - Mining partners, community outreach
mbekhet - Web dev
Mortimer452 - Math wizard, crypto expert, wiki curator
Nielsg93 - Community and social outreach and web dev
sebastien1234 - Wiki curator
snipsnoop - Wallet compilation

MEOW

LEAFCOIN

"CRYPTOCURRENCY WITH GREEN INTENTIONS"

Scrypt Proof of Work

BLOCK REWARD DISTRIBUTION SCHEDULE TABLE

Block Phase	Block Number	Reward	Date of Initial Block
Pre-mine	1-100	1-1,000,000	~23rd of January 2014
Initial Phase	101-14,999	1-1,000,000	~24th of January 2014
1st Halving	15,000-29,999	1-500,000	~2nd of February 2014
2nd Halving	30,000-44,999	1-250,000	~13th of February 2014
3rd Halving	45,000-59,999	1-125,000	~23rd of February 2014
——————--	——————--	——————--	——————-——
6th Halving	90,000-104,999	1-15,625	~26th of March 2014
7th Halving	105,000-119,999	1-7,812	~6th of April 2014
8th Halving	120,000-	3,500	~16th of April 2014

LEAF

LEAFCOIN

"CRYPTOCURRENCY WITH GREEN INTENTIONS"
"NEW GENERATION INTERNET CURRENCY"

SPECIFICATION

Symbol:	LEAF
Launched (Founder):	24th of January 2014 (11.20pm EST) ("mcg")
Hashing Algorithm:	Scrypt
Timestamping Algorithm:	Proof of Work
Address Begins With:	f
Total Coins:	21 billion
Block Time/Difficulty Retarget:	60 seconds/60 seconds (KGW)
Coins per Block:	(see the first page)
Confirmations per Transaction:	Unknown
Pre-mine:	Yes (First 100 blocks)

- First block was mined on the 23rd of January 2014.

- The starting difficulty was 0.000.

- First difficulty re-target algorithm used to re-target every 240 minutes.

- Difficulty retargets every block using Kimoto's Gravity Well.

- The block reward halved every 15,000 blocks, initially an average of 500,000 per block at launch.

- The first 100 blocks were pre-mined for checkpoints and giveaways.

http://leafco.in   (Official Website)
http://explorer.leafco.in   (Block Explorer)
http://forum.leafco.in   (Official Forum)
http://foundation.leafco.in   (Leafcoin Foundation)

LEAF

HISTORY

"CRYPTOCURRENCY WITH GREEN INTENTIONS"
"NEW GENERATION INTERNET CURRENCY"

LEAF

On the 24th of January 2014, "mcg" announced Leafcoin on Bitcointalk. On the same day, the first Leafcoin block explorer (http://cryptexplorer.com/chain/Leafcoin) was created thanks to "candidakefyr". On the 25th, the Leafcoin Facebook group and Twitter page were founded. One day later, "mcg" realised that the coin had a 61 billion coin cap, caused by a mathematical mistake. Leafcoin was initially meant to have a 21 billion cap. This was corrected soon after. On the 27th, the trading pair LEAF/LTC was the first exchange pair ever for LEAF on Fresh Market.

On the 1st of February, it was listed on Coinmarketcap. Leafcoin reached an all time high of about $2,014,889 in terms of market cap on the 4th of February. At this peak, one LEAF was worth 0.015 mLTC according to Cryptsy. This was clearly influence by its initial price listing on that exchange. On the 8th, users had to upgrade their wallet clients to the new "Gravity Fix 3rd Client". This update implemented Kimoto's Gravity Well as the difficulty re-target algorithm. It fixed the problems caused by multipool attacks. KGW became active on the 10th at block number 18,818. Before this date, the difficulty of the network re-targeted every 240 blocks. On the 19th, the LEAF Foundation (www.foundation.leafco.in) was created. On the 27th, a logo competition began.

On the 7th of March, the logo contest ended. On the 8th, the Android Wallet App became available on Google Play and the new Leafcoin logo designed by "LEO whit cryptoworld.eu picove" was chosen via a vote. One day later, the official Leafcoin forum (http://forum.leafco.in) was founded. On the 13th, a new Bitcointalk thread was created by "mcg".

On the 4th of April, the Leafcoin price ticker app (Android) became available on Google Play.

On the 29th of June, after many weeks of absence on the Bitcointalk thread, "mcg" returned to announce future plans to change the coin's timestamping algorithm to proof of stake. This never materialised and the coin appears to have been abandoned by its two developers, "mcg" and "aaron_m".

www.facebook.com/leafcoin
www.reddit.com/r/leafcoin
www.twitter.com/leafcoin

LEAF IS A PEER-TO-PEER DECENTRALIZED OPEN SOURCE CURRENCY WITH FAST TRANSACTION TIMES.

The original LEAF coin logo

MISCELLANEOUS

The developers describe themselves as small and dedicated.

The developers also implemented centralised checkpoints in order to increase network security.

A new logo was chosen by the community.

LEAF Foundation is a partner of the WWF. One of its current goals is to raise funds to help tackle deforestation. (www.foundation.leafco.in).

A cryptocurrency with green intentions, fast block halvings and fast block times.

EXCHANGES

FreshMarket (added on ~27/01/14)
CoinMarket (added on ~28/01/14)
Coined Up (added on ~31/01/14)
Poloniex (added on ~01/02/14)
Beedui (added on ~02/02/14)
Cryptsy (added on ~04/02/14)
CryptX (added on ~08/02/14)
Swisscex (added on ~10/02/14)
Newaltex (added on ~12/02/14)
pmtocoins (added on ~09/03/14)
Cryptokk (added on ~11/03/14)

LEAF TEAM

"mcg"—Founder
"aaron_m" - Developer

LEAF

LITECOIN

"COMMERCE AT THE SPEED OF LITE"

Scrypt Proof of Work

BLOCK REWARD DISTRIBUTION SCHEDULE TABLE

Block Phase	Block Number	Reward	Date of Initial Block
Pre-mine	1-3	50	~8th of October 2011
First Phase	4-839,999	50	~13th of October 2011
1st Halving	840,000-1,679,999	25	~10th of October 2015
2nd Halving	1,680,000-2,519,999	12.5	~7th of October 2019
3rd Halving	2,520,000-3,359,999	6.25	~5th of October 2023
4th Halving	3,360,000-4,199,999	3.125	~2nd of October 2027

And so on...

The block reward continues to halve every 840,000 blocks (~every four years)

LTC

LITECOIN

"COMMERCE AT THE SPEED OF LITE"

SPECIFICATION

Symbol:	LTC, Ł
Launched (Founder):	13th of October 2011 03:00 GMT ("coblee")
Hashing Algorithm:	Scrypt
Timestamping Algorithm:	Proof of Work
Address Begins With:	L
Total coins:	84 million
Block Time/Difficulty Retarget:	2.5 minutes/2016 blocks
Coins per Block:	(see the first page)
Confirmations per Transaction:	4
Pre-mine:	First 3 blocks (150 coins)

- Open source software project released under the MIT/X11 license.

- Difficulty adjusts every 2016 blocks, approximately every 3.5 days.

- LTC was pre-mined in order to test whether the genesis block was valid.

- Block reward halves every 840,000 blocks.

- Litecoin was forked directly form the Bitcoin source code.

- Starting difficulty was 0.00024414 (same as a past coin called Tenebrix).

- The Litecoin network is scheduled to produce four times as many currency units as Bitcoin.

https://litecoin.org/ (Official Website)
http://block-explorer.com/ (Block Explorer)
https://litecointalk.org/ (Official Forum)

LTC

HISTORY

"COMMERCE AT THE SPEED OF LITE"

On the 7th of October 2011, Charles Lee, a former Google employee, released Litecoin via open-source client on GitHub. Some users joined Litecoin IRC chat to create a real alternative currency to Bitcoin. Two days later, "coblee" (Charles Lee) pre-announced the coin on Bitcointalk. On the next day, the source code and the Windows client were released. Users on the Litecoin Bitcointalk thread voted on the best time to launch the coin on the 12th of October. Also on the 12th, the official website was created thanks to "terrytibbs". A vote was 39 out of 91 in favour of launch at 3am GMT on the 13th of October 2011.

On the 26th of June 2012, user "smoothie" bought a pizza from Papa John's in Honolulu for 3,500 LTC. At the time LTC was trading for about $0.005 per coin on BTC-e.

In June 2013, there were rumours that Mt. Gox would add LTC to their exchange. This never occurred.

On the 30th of July 2013, Charlie Lee joined the Coinbase (a Bitcoin transaction processing site) team.

On the 2nd of October 2013, the price of one LTC went as low as $1.11 on BTC-e. On the 31st of October, the trading website Litecoinglobal ceased all services.

On the 18th of November 2013, the price of Litecoin went from just over $4 to approx. $9.50. On the 28th of November 2013, after a 400% increase over the preceding three days, Litecoin reached an all time high at a market cap of about $1.1 billion. At this peak, it was worth $48.48 according to BTC-e.

On the 15th of December 2013, a client (V 0.8.6.1) was released. It implemented a 20x reduction in transaction fees as well as adding extra security parameters.

On the 13th of January 2014, Forbes.com wrote an article about Litecoin titled "A $100 Worth Of Litecoin A Year Ago Is Worth $30,000 Today". On the 19th, the Litecoin Android wallet was released. This new release replaced the old Android client which contained major security issues. On the 26th of January, Charlie Lee gave a speech at the Miami Bitcoin Conference.

On the 12th of March 2014, the price of Litecoin spiked due to the announcement by Huobi that they would be adding LTC to their exchange. Huobi was the busiest exchange in China at the time.

On the 4th of April 2014, Benz and Beamer auto dealership announced it sold a Tesla Model SP85 to an anonymous customer for 5,447 LTC (~$90,000 at the time of purchase.). The dealership processed the transaction in partnership with GoCoin. It was the largest amount of litecoins used in a single purchase recorded at the time. On the 7th, Charles Lee talked to the co-founder of Dogecoin, Jack Palmer, about making the case of merged mining between LTC and DOGE. Also in April, a client (V 0.8.7.1) as well as a new Litecoin Electrum client (a lightweight wallet for Litecoin in beta test state) were released.

On the 8th of May 2014, a Electrum Wallet (V 1.9.8.2) Release Candidate was released. On the 28th of May, another Electrum Litecoin Wallet (V 1.9.8.4) was released. Another version of the Electrum Litecoin wallet was released on the 20th of August 2014.

On the 11th of September, Litecoin began merge mining with Dogecoin.

www.facebook.com/litecoincommunity
www.reddit.com/r/litecoin
www.twitter.com/LitecoinProject

"coblee" bitcointalk avatar

MISCELLANEOUS

Charlie Lee explains that Litecoin was never intended to be a Bitcoin replacement. Instead he intended Litecoin to complement Bitcoin in the same way that silver complements gold.

First cryptocurrency to successfully use Scrypt and a faster block generation rate.

The Litecoin project is currently maintained by a core group of 6 software developers, led by Charles Lee, with a large community that is growing in support.

BTC-e has been the main trading exchange for Litecoin over three years.

Before Litecoin, Charles Lee actually tried to launch some other cryptocurrencies. His first, Fairbrix, was a clone of another coin called Tenebrix. It turned out to be a fiasco.

EXCHANGES

BTC-e (added on ~16/10/11)
Virurex (added on ~22/10/11)
Cryptsy (added on ~20/05/13)
Bitfinex (added on ~24/05/13)
C-Cex (added on ~16/01/14)
Swisscex (added on ~08/02/14)
Bittrex (added on ~13/02/14)
MintPal (added on ~23/02/14)
BTCChina (added on ~06/03/14)
Gamblex (added on ~12/03/14)
AGX (added on ~15/03/14)
Huobi (added on ~19/03/14)
Coin-Swap (added on ~30/04/14)

LTC

MAXCOIN

"BRINGING DIGITAL CURRENCY TO THE WORLD"

SHA-3 Keccak Proof of Work

BLOCK REWARD DISTRIBUTION SCHEDULE TABLE

Block Phase	Block Number	Reward	Date of Initial Block
Initial Phase	1-139,999	96	~6th of February 2014
1st Halving	140,000-600,000	48	~27th of March 2014
Third Phase	600,001-2,702,399	16	~5th of September 2014
2nd Halving	2,702,400-4,804,799	8	~5th of September 2018
3rd Halving	4,804,800-6,907,199	4	~5th of September 2022
4th Halving	6,907,200-9,009,599	2	~5th of September 2026
5th Halving	9,009,600-11,111,999	1	~5th of September 2030

The block reward will halve roughly every four years from the 5th of September 2014.
This is about every ~2,102,400 blocks.

MAXCOIN

"BRINGING DIGITAL CURRENCY TO THE WORLD"

SPECIFICATION

Symbol:	MAX
Launched (Founder):	6th of February 2014 (7.30pm GMT) (Max Keiser)
Hashing Algorithm:	SHA-3 Keccak
Timestamping Algorithm:	Proof of Work
Address Begins With:	m
Total coins:	100 million
Block Time/Difficulty Retarget:	60 seconds/KGW
Coins per Block:	(see the first page)
Confirmations per Transaction:	Unknown
Pre-mine:	None

- Uses an advanced hashing algorithm called SHA-3 Keccak which is ASIC resistant, so current Bitcoin ASICs and the upcoming Scrypt ASICs are useless on this coin. MAX is mined with CPUs.

- Since block 200, difficulty retargets at a variable rate as a result of Kimoto's Gravity Well.

- The block reward was initially 96 with a maximum coin cap of ~250 million.

- Low-difficulty instamining was tackled with a fast retarget rate up until block 200.

- Not a fork of DOGE.

- Checkpointing exists to provide additional blockchain security.

- No transaction fees.

http://maxcoin.co.uk	(Official Website)
http://max.cryptoexplore.com	(Block Explorer)
http://www.maxtalk.org/	(Official Forum)

MAX

HISTORY

"BRINGING DIGITAL CURRENCY TO THE WORLD"

On the 6th of January 2014, the Maxcoin Facebook group was founded. The Twitter page was founded on the 27th of January. The official website was also created before the launch. On the 28th, The Keiser Report on RT broadcasted an interview with the Maxcoin development team. Maxcoin was announced on the 29th on Bitcointalk by "maxcoinproject" in order to facilitate a fair launch. The developers set a hard deadline for this launch in order not to disadvantage the miners.

After a delayed launch due to issues concerning huge forum traffic, Maxcoin finally launched on the 6th of February. This was not the initially intended launch date. Maxcoin was initially listed on the exchange called Coins-e as the trading pair MAX/BTC on the same day. On the 12th, it was added to Coinmarketcap.com. Maxcoin reached an all time high of about $6,579,903 in terms of market cap three days later. At this peak, one MAX was worth 0.004848 BTC according to Bter. On the 21st, Maxcoin was added to the gift card service pock.io. On the 27th, Maxcoin was added to www.coinpayments.net.

On the 20th of March, a reduction in the block reward was announced with a new coin cap of approximately 100 million. A new wallet client (Macoin 0.9.0) was released ready for users to install before block number 140,000. On the 25th, MAX/USD became available on the exchange Prelude. Two days later, the block reward halved from 96 to 48 coins as well as the reduction to a 100 million coin cap. This decision was taken as a result of calls from the community to address the issue of excessive coin inflation.

On the 2nd of April, the official forum (www.maxtalk.org) was launched. On the 4th, it was announced that a hard fork was to be introduced at block number 177,500 in order to fix the time warp exploit in Kimoto's Gravity Well. The wallet client update was Maxcoin (V 0.9.1).

On the 8th of May, Prypto released MAX scratch cards that hold 20 MAX.

On the 23rd of June, the Maxcoin news website (http://maxcoinnews.net) went live. Six days later, an auction site (www.maxbay.eu/) was launched.

On the 13th of July, the Maxcoin Silver Cryptobullion campaign on StartJoin sold out. The project exceeded $114,000, after just 14 days, with every reward being claimed.

On the 29th of August, a client (V 0.9.2.0) was released. It had to be installed before a hard fork at block number 600,001.

On the 5th of September, the block time increased from 30 seconds to 60 seconds, the block reward reduced from 48 to 16 and the total number of coins to be mined remained at 100,000,000 The block reward halving interval was increased from 1 year to 4 years. A checkpointing protocol was implemented in order to provide additional security to the blockchain. On the 13th, a client (V 0.9.3.1) was released. It was mandatory as it fixed wallet synchronisation issues and incorporated the new current Maxcoin logo into the client.

On the 13th of October, after extensive development, the official website and block explorer were improved. A StartJoin campaign raised $574 ($500 target) to help fund the development.

www.facebook.com/MaxKeiserCoin
www.reddit.com/r/maxcoin
www.twitter.com/maxcoinproject

maxcoin

MISCELLANEOUS

Maxcoin was founded and inspired by the journalist called Max Keiser.

The Maxcoin development team consists of students/staff from Bristol University.

During the launch phase, the Maxcoin website and its corresponding Bitcointalk thread could not cope due to high volumes of traffic. This delayed the launch.

The people most likely to participate in Maxcoin are those who view the Keiser Report on Russia Today.

Max Keiser uses the MAX he mines in addition to some BTC to fund cryptocurrency startups and apps via StartJOIN.

EXCHANGES

Coins-e (added on ~06/02/14)
Bittylicious (added on ~06/02/14)
mcxNOW (added on ~07/02/14)
Cryptorush (added on ~07/02/14)
Poloniex (added on ~08/02/14)
Bter (added on ~11/02/14)
Cryptsy (added on ~15/02/14)
Swisscex (added on ~21/02/14)
AGX (added on ~15/03/14)
Prelude (added on ~17/03/14)
Bleutrade (added on ~25/03/14)
Comkort (added on ~28/03/14)
Atomic Trade (added on ~21/04/14)
Coinnext (added on ~21/05/14)
C-Cex (added on ~10/07/14)
Bittrex (added on ~02/08/14)

MAX TEAM

Alex—Digital Arts and Media
Luke—Lead Developer

Mike—Market Research and Economic Advisor
John—Marketing

MAX

MAZACOIN

"NATIONAL CURRENCY OF THE TRADITIONAL LAKOTA NATION"

SHA-256 Proof of Work

BLOCK REWARD DISTRIBUTION SCHEDULE TABLE

Block Phase	Block Number	Reward	Date of Initial Block
Pre-mine	1-10,000	5,000	~7th of February 2014
Initial Phase	10,001-99,999	5,000	~22nd of February 2014
Second Phase	100,000-1,049,999	1,000	~4th of July 2014
1st Halving	1,050,000-1,999,999	500	~12th of February 2018
2nd Halving	2,000,000-2,949,999	250	~23rd of September 2021
3rd Halving	2,950,000-3,899,999	125	~5th of May 2025
4th Halving	3,900,000-4,849,999	62.5	~14th of December 2028

An so on ...
1.45 billion coins after 4 years and 2.34 Billion after 18 years.

MZC

MAZACOIN

"NATIONAL CURRENCY OF THE TRADITIONAL LAKOTA NATION"
"STRENGTH THROUGH UNITY"

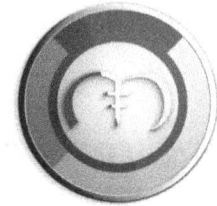

SPECIFICATION

Symbol:	MZC, m
Launched (Founders):	22nd of February 2014 (Payu Harris, Anonymous Pirate)
Hashing Algorithm:	SHA-256
Timestamping Algorithm:	Proof of Work
Address Begins With:	M
Total Coins:	(see below)
Block Time/Difficulty Retarget:	120 seconds/Dark Gravity Wave 3
Coins per Block:	(see the first page)
Confirmations per Transaction:	5
Pre-mine:	50 million (Two Phase)

- It was launched to the public at 12 noon ET USA on the 22nd of February 2014.

- Version 0.8.1 BETA 1.2 Treaty Edition.

- It is a new fork based on the sourcecode of Zetacoin 0.8.99.

- ASIC mining compatible.

- Difficulty used to retarget every 4 blocks depending on the previous 90 blocks before block number 100,000. From this block, it began to use the Dark Gravity Wave 3 difficulty re-targeting algorithm.

- The block reward started at 5,000 and was planned to halve every 241,920 blocks (approximately every 12 months) until the reward is 1 MZC per block. After block 100,000, the block reward was reduced to 1,000. The block reward halves every 950,000 blocks from block number 100,000.

- There is no maximum coin supply. A supply of about 2.398 billion coins (initially 2.4192 billion) will be mined after about 36 years (initially 5 years) and then a yearly inflation thereafter.

http://mazacoin.org	(Official Website)
http://mazacha.in	(Block Explorer)
http://mazatalk.com/	(Community Website)

MZC

HISTORY

"NATIONAL CURRENCY OF THE TRADITIONAL LAKOTA NATION"
"STRENGTH THROUGH UNITY"

On the 26th of December 2013, the official Facebook group (www.facebook.com/Mazacoin) was founded. One day later, the Twitter page was created. Both these pages were created well in advance of the launch.

On the 26th of January 2014, it was announced that Mazacoin would be available for download and ready for miners on the 15th of February. On the 29th, the first Mazacoin address was generated at 1pm ET USA (MChYQ8ztLazpXBJAHJEC5A1SJAuoTP329d). One day later, the first official MZC white paper was released.

On the 7th of February, the first block (genesis) was mined (9:30am ET USA) and so the mining of the pre-mine began. Also, the first transaction took place 187 minutes later. Two phases of pre-mine were accumulated. One half of the pre-mine is the National Reserve Fund from which coins are used to help fund local ventures. The other half is used to fund individuals (1,000 MZC), businesses (10,000 MZC) and non-profit organisations (50,000 MZC), the MZC Tribal Trust. On the 22nd, the Ubuntu wallet client and the MZC source code became available to download. On the 26th, MZC was added to the site Coinmarketcap.

On the 3rd of March, Payu Harris gave a speech at the Bitcoin Center in New York. Mazacoin reached an all time high of about $11,298,097 in terms of market cap on the 4th of March. One day later, the volume of Mazacoin trading on the exchange called MintPal in its first 24 hours reached 1,500 BTC. On the 6th, the MZC/LTC market on MintPal opened. On the 10th, the Mazacoin Android wallet app was released for download via the official website. A Mazacoin marketplace went live on day later. On the 25th, David Mills (Director Oglala Sioux Tribe) put forward a resolution to the Tribal E&BD Committee. Their future decision on Mazacoin will depend on its on going success and development. On the 28th, it went live on the payment processing platform called coinpayments.net.

On the 3rd of April, the current official website (www.mazacoin.org) went live.

On the 29th of May, "owlhooter" joined the development team. On the 30th of May, the MZC/LTC trading pair was closed on MintPal.

On the 20th of June, it was announced that a future hard fork would occur at block number 100,000. One day later, a client (V 9.0.1) was released ready for users to install before this hard fork. On the 22nd, a new Bitcointalk thread was created by "Skirmant". Five days later, a new block explorer (www.mazacha.in) was released.

On the 4th of July, block number 100,000 was reached. The block reward was reduced from 5,000 to 1,000. One reason why they decided to slow the rate of inflation was due to longer than anticipated adoption by the Lakota. The difficulty retargeting algorithm was also changed to Dark Gravity Wave (DGW3) in order to create more consistent times of blocks on the blockchain.

On the 5th of August, the first "Mazacoin Weekly Report" was released on the official website. One day later, the Mazacoin reddit tipbot went live. On the 25th, a Mazacoin documentary produced by Bianca Consunji & Evan Engel of Mashable previewed at the Bitcoin Center NYC.

www.facebook.com/Mazacoin
www.reddit.com/r/mazacoin
www.twitter.com/MazaCoin

MISCELLANEOUS

Mazacoin is the official cryptocurrency for the Native American Nation based in Dakota, USA.

It was one of the first sovereign national cryptocurrency to be released alongside Auroracoin. It was announced via a Mazacoin press release on the 27th of December at noon ET USA.

Both pre-mines have their own publicly seen wallet addresses.

Payu Harris founded the BTC Oyate Initiative which facilitates a close working relationship between the traditional Lakota Nation and the developers.

Two major developer objectives are to see Mazacoin alleviate poverty and augment the sovereignty of the Lakota Nation.

First transaction (1,000 MZC) at 12:37pm ET USA 07/02/2014.

EXCHANGES

Cryptorush (added on ~23/02/14)
MintPal (added on ~04/03/14)
Atomic Trade (added on ~04/03/14)
Swisscex (added on ~06/03/14)
Cryptsy (added on ~07/03/14)
Poloniex (added on ~09/03/14)
AllCrypt (added on ~11/03/14)
Coined Up (added on ~23/03/14)
Bittrex (added on ~23/03/14)
LazyCoins (added on ~01/08/14)

MZC TEAM

Payu Harris - Creator, Media Relations

Tom Donaldson (owlhooter) - Lead Core Developer

Rob Nelson (guruvan) - Project Coordinator

Tyler Willis (Kefkius) – Core Development,

Xendarboh (sensorii) – Core Development

Skirmantas – Core development (Android/JS)

Sarah Verbanac (bananalotus), Social Media

George Magaris – Graphic Design

Tomis – Graphic Design

MZC

MEGACOIN

"YOUR GLOBAL CURRENCY"

Scrypt Proof of Work

BLOCK REWARD DISTRIBUTION SCHEDULE TABLE

Block Phase	Block Number	Reward	Date of Initial Block
Initial Phase	1-20,999	500	~1st of June 2013
1st Halving	21,000-41,999	250	~22nd of June 2013
2nd Halving	42,000-62,999	125	~28th of July 2013
Second Phase	63,000-83,999	75	~13th of September 2013
Third Phase	84,000-104,999	50	~20th of October 2013
3rd Halving	105,000-524,999	25	~25th of November 2013
4th Halving	525,000-944,999	12.5	~10th of November 2015
5th Halving	945,000-1,364,999	6.25	~30th of October 2017
6th Halving	1,365,000-1,784,999	3.125	~20th of October 2019

And so on...

MEC

MEGACOIN

"YOUR GLOBAL CURRENCY"

SPECIFICATION

Symbol:	MEC
Launched (Founder):	1st of June 2013 (Dr. Kimoto Chan, "kimoto")
Hashing Algorithm:	Scrypt
Timestamping Algorithm:	Proof of Work
Address Begins With:	M
Total Coins:	42 million
Block Time/Difficulty Retarget:	2.5 minutes/every block (KGW)
Coins per Block:	(see the first page)
Confirmations per Transaction:	5
Pre-mine:	None

- 21 million MEC were mined in the initial adoption phase in the first 5 months.

- Every 21,000 blocks (~1 month) the reward stepped down from 500, 250, 125, 75, 50.

- Every 420,000 blocks (two years), the reward starts at 25 and is halved each period.

- Through the next few decades the remaining 21 million will be generated.

- 10.5 million coins come from the first two years of 420,000 blocks.

- Megacoins are mined by users at a set rate for decades into the future.

- Uses the Scrypt proof of work algorithm so it can be mined with CPU and GPU.

- The difficulty retargeting time was initially 22.5 minutes before KGW was implemented.

http://megacoin.co.nz   (Official Website)
http://mec.blockr.io/   (Block Explorer)
https://forum.megacoin.co.nz/   (Official Forum)

MEC

HISTORY

"YOUR GLOBAL CURRENCY"

MEC

On the 29th of May 2013, Megacoin was announced on Bitcointalk by user "kimoto".

On the 1st of June, the first block (genesis block) was mined. On the 5th, the source code for Megacoin was released by "kimoto". On the same day, "kimoto" offered a 2,500 MEC bounty to anyone in the community who created a working faucet. Within 24 hours, user "r3wt" created one. On the 13th, an updated client (V 0.8.991) including a CPU fix became available and "MobGod" created the first MEC block explorer. On the 17th, an updated client (V 0.8.992) was released which implemented new checkpoints. On the 20th, a logo competition, which lasted about four days, ended. The winner, who actually won first, third and fifth prize, was user "ohiwastedmylif". He received a total prize of 4,000 MEC. On the 22nd, a new Bitcointalk thread was launched by "kimoto".

On the 3rd of July, the official website (www.megacoin.co.nz) was launched. On the 7th, it was added to Coinmarketcap.com. On the 19th, a new updated client (V 0.8.993) was released.

On the 7th of August, a new updated client (V 0.8.994) was released. On the 28th, "kimoto" created the new Kimoto Gravity Well difficulty retargeting algorithm. Also, the participation of "ohiwastedmylif" in the community ended.

On the 8th of September, a mandatory client update (V 0.8.995) was released before a fork in the blockchain. It implemented KGW as the difficulty retargeting algorithm. Users had to update before block number 63,000 in order to be on the correct chain thereafter (KGW started at block 63,005). On the 12th, a Mac client was created by "maxpower" who received a reward of 5,000 MEC as thanks. On the 13th, another update to the wallet was released (V 0.8.996) just before the fork occurred on the same day.

On the 7th of November, the official Megacoin Twitter page was launched. On the 22nd, the market cap of Megacoin went above $1 million for the first time. Eight days later, Megacoin reached an all time high of about $51,805,807 in terms of market cap. At this peak, one MEC was worth 0.0024 BTC ($2.46) according to Cryptsy.

On the 15th of January 2014, the first MEC/USD trades were made at the Coin Market exchange. On the 22nd, Megacoin was discussed on 3 News in New Zealand. By the 28th, eight other alts had adopted KGW.

On the 5th of February, 21 alt coins had adopted KGW. On the 9th, the Megacoin Android wallet was released in beta state. One week later, a Megacoin marketing fund was launched on the official forum. By the end of February, over one hundred alt coins had adopted the KGW algorithm.

On the 23rd of April, a new Megacoin paper wallet generator became available via the forum.

On the 25th of June, over 250 other alt coins had adopted the KGW algorithm.

On the 7th of August, two YouTube videos were uploaded titled "Megacoin Marketing Fund".

On the 13th of October, the trading pair MEC/XRP (XRP is the symbol of Ripple) was added to the exchange called Cryptsy.

www.facebook.com/megacoin.world
www.reddit.com/r/megacoin/
www.twitter.com/mega_coin

Original Logo

Kimoto Gravity Well

MISCELLANEOUS

There has been controversy over who Dr.Kimoto really is. Is it Kim Dot Com from New Zealand?

Below is a quote from "kimoto":

"That was the day I invented time-dilated difficulty gravitational wells. The black holes of difficulty formulas! I remember it vividly. I was standing on the edge of my toilet about to upload a standard fork, the porcelain was wet, I slipped, hit my head on the sink, and when I came to I had a revelation! A vision! A picture in my head! A picture of this (Kimoto's Gravity)!"

The first known physical transaction of Megacoin was on the 7th of September 2013. 5,000 MEC for a pizza. On the 1st of December 2103, that value equated to about $12,750.

EXCHANGES

Cryptsy (added on ~11/06/13)
CoinEx (added on ~31/07/13)
PhenixEx (added on ~25/08/13)
Bter (added on ~31/08/13)
Coin Market (added on ~15/01/14)
LiteBit (added on ~08/07/14)
Bleutrade (added on ~04/11/14)

MEC TEAM

Developer—Dr. Kimoto Chan
PR Marketer—Alienwalkerx
PR Marketer—nbk
PR Marketer—Janek

Community Spokesperson—Alienwalkerx
Community Spokesperson—ethought
Community Spokesperson—MegaMike
Community Spokesperson—BAHcontactKCK
Community Spokesperson—Itscrazybro

MEC

MINTCOIN

"START MINTING"

Scrypt Proof of Stake

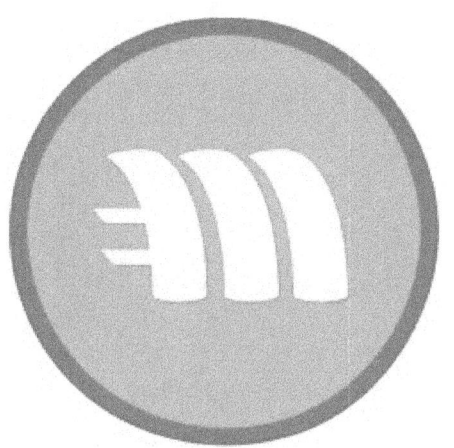

BLOCK REWARD DISTRIBUTION SCHEDULE TABLE

Block Phase	Block Number	Reward	Date of Initial Block
Initial Phase	1-20,160	100,000-900,000	~6th of February 2014
1st Halving	20,161-40,320	50,000-450,000	~13th of February 2014
2nd Halving	40,321-60,480	25,000-225,000	~20th of February 2014
3rd Halving	60,481-80,640	12,500-112,500	~27th of February 2014
4th Halving	80,641-100,800	6,250-56,250	~6th of March 2014
5th Halving	100,801-120,960	3,125-28,125	~13th of March 2014
Last Phase	120,961-220,000	1	~20th of March 2014

The interest rates on MINT held in one's wallet for generating further coins are:

20% for the first year, 15% for the second year.
10% for the third year and then 5% for the succeeding years.

MINTCOIN

"START MINTING"
"A GREEN ALTERNATIVE"

SPECIFICATION

Symbol:	MINT (originally MNT)
Launched (Founder):	6th of February 2014 (7pm GMT) ("mintcointeam")
Hashing Algorithm:	Scrypt
Timestamping Algorithm:	Proof of Stake
Address Begins With:	M
Coin Total:	70 billion
Block Time/Difficulty Retarget:	30 seconds/KGW
Coins per Block:	(see the first page)
Confirmations per Transaction:	4
Pre-mine:	1% (all been used for initial coin growth)

- It used a faster proof of work distribution mechanism to distribute the initial coins.

- The block reward halved approximately every week for the first 5 weeks since it launched. After this initial 5 weeks, MINT is now solely generated via Proof of Stake. As a result, it is now considered a pure PoS cryptocurrency.

- Proof of work block rewards ceased at block number 220,000 on the 2nd of April 2014.

- Kimoto's Gravity Well is used to regulate the difficulty.

- A total of 70 billion coins is set to be distributed in a four year period.

- PoS will start after at least 20 days of holding of the coins in the wallet (Investor friendly)

- 50 confirmations for minted blocks .

http://mintcoin.cc   (Official Website)
http://mint.blockx.info/get/chain/MintCoin   (Block Explorer)
http://www.mintcointalk.com/   (Official Forum)

MINT

HISTORY

"START MINTING"

"A GREEN ALTERNATIVE"

Before the launch of the coin, the Facebook group was founded on the 1st of February 2014. On the 5th, user "mintcointeam" announced MINT on Bitcointalk. On the 8th, the first bock explorer (http://mintcoin-explorer.info) was created. On the 18th, a Windows client (V 1.3) was released (not mandatory) in order to address many issues. One the same day, the MINT official forum was launched. One day later, Coinmarketcap.com added the coin. Another Windows client (V 1.4) was released on the 22nd, but once again, this was not a mandatory update. On the 23rd, the MINT/LTC market was added to MintPal. On the 26th, proof of stake began. Mintcoin reached an all time high of about $4,422,264 in terms of market cap on the 27th. At this peak, one MINT was worth 0.00044 mBTC according to Cryptsy.

On the 5th of March, MINT went live on the consumer platform Moolah. On the 9th, a client (V 1.5) was released with the latest checkpoints (not mandatory). Three days later, the new current MINT logo was chosen for immediate use. The winning design (triple-bar) was courtesy of "pixibug". Five days later, version 1.6 of the Windows Wallet was released with this new logo incorporated. On the 25th, the trading pair MINT/USD became available on the Prelude exchange.

On the 2nd of April, a mandatory client (V 1.6) became available that made proof of work obsolete after block 220,000. One day later, the MAC OS X Wallet was released.

The "Sonoma County Redwood Reforest" campaign by the Mintcoin Fund reached its 100 supporter target on ThunderClap at 12pm EDT on the 5th of May. On the 22nd, the MAC OS X wallet (V 1.9.1) was released one month after its Windows equivalent was. On the 30th, MintPal closed the MINT/LTC trading pair.

On the 6th of June, the Multicoin Tipping App on Facebook started out with MINT as a tipping option. On the 14th, a new block explorer (mint.blockexplorer.com) was created. Four days later, the MINT Reddit tipbot began to function. On the 21st, a new updated Windows wallet (V 1.10) was released with the MAC OS X following two days later.

On the 3rd of July, altcoinauctions.com started to accept MINT. A song called "Ballin' on the Mintcoin" was made by @mclars one week later. It can be found on YouTube. On the 18th, the MINT developer "mintcointeam" handed over responsibility of the coin to the community. Jessica Hartman "CryptoMommy" is now the head of MINT development.

On the 1st of September, a campaign began to help sponsor 500 students in Gambia. It is called the Keepod initiative. Its aim is to raise money to supply students in that country with personalised computers and internet access.

www.facebook.com/MintCoin
www.reddit.com/r/MintCoin
www.twitter.com/MintcoinTeam

The Original MINT coin logo

MISCELLANEOUS

Mint is a fast growing and extending plant.

Minting is the process of earning interest by holding coins.

One day after the launch, the symbol was changed from MNT to the current MINT.

Mintcoin Fund is the world's first legally-registered NGO for a cryptocurrency.

EXCHANGES

Newaltex (added on ~09/02/14)
MintPal (added on ~09/02/14)
CoinMarket (added on ~19/02/14)
Poloniex (added on ~20/02/14)
Cryptorush (added on ~21/02/14)
Cryptsy (added on ~24/02/14)
OpenEx (added on ~24/02/14)
C-Cex (added on ~24/02/14)
Bter (added on ~24/02/14)
Bittrex (added on ~11/03/14)
Cryptokopen (added on ~13/03/14)
Prelude (added on ~17/03/14)
Coined Up (added on ~23/03/14)
AGX (added on ~27/03/14)
Bleutrade (added on ~07/04/14)
Vault of Satoshi (added on ~10/04/14)

MINT TEAM

"mintcointeam"—Founder

MINT

MOONCOIN

"YOU KNOW WHERE IT'S HEADED"

Scrypt Proof of Work

BLOCK REWARD DISTRIBUTION SCHEDULE TABLE

Block Phase	Block Number	Reward	Date of Initial Block
Initial Phase	1-100,000	1-2,000,000	~30th of December 2013
Second Phase	100,001-200,000	1-1,000,000	~8th of May 2014
Third Phase	200,001-250,000	1-600,000	~20th of August 2014
Fourth Phase	250,001-300,000	1-350,000	~12th of October 2014
Fifth Phase	300,001-350,000	1-175,000	~3rd of December 2014
Sixth Phase	350,001-375,000	1-100,000	~24th of January 2015
Seventh Phase	375,001-384,400	1-50,000	~19th of February 2015

All future blocks after 384,400 are each fixed at a block reward of 29,531 MOON.

MOON

MOONCOIN

"YOU KNOW WHERE IT'S HEADED"

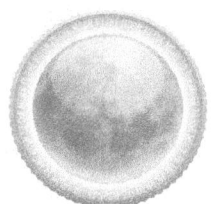

SPECIFICATION

Symbol:	MOON
Launched (Founder):	30th of December 2013 (1pm EST) ("deaconboogie")
Hashing Algorithm:	Scrypt
Timestamping Algorithm:	Proof of Work
Address Begins With:	2
Total Coins:	384.4 billion
Block Time/Difficulty Retarget:	90 seconds/KGW
Coins per Block:	(see below)
Confirmations per Transaction:	Unknown
Pre-mine:	None

- On the 21st of July 2014, it was the 45th anniversary of the lunar landing by the Apollo 11 astronauts. On this date, Mooncoin was scheduled to release one MOON for every USD spent on the Apollo space program at an accelerated rate of 25.4 billion MOON. This was delayed due to slow average block generation times.

- Every block number based on the lunar cycle will be awarded a 2x payout bonus!

- Before the change to KGW, the difficulty re-targeting occurred every 8 hours (every 320 blocks).

- Between blocks 193,076-203,157, bonus blocks were generated to celebrate the 45th anniversary of Apollo 11. This began on the 13th of August 2014. So the Mooncoin-Apollo-phase came to an end at block number 203,157 on the 23rd of August 2014.

- Other specials will come in future releases.

http://mooncoin.wordpress.com/   (Official Site)
http://www.moonchain.net/chain/Mooncoin   (Block Explorer)

MOON

HISTORY

"YOU KNOW WHERE IT'S HEADED"

User "deaconboogie" announced MOON on Bitcointalk on the 28th of December 2013. It was launched on the 30th. The official Facebook group was also founded on the 30th. It's developers said that no coins were pre-mined, despite there being some people who said otherwise. On the last day of 2013, MOON/BTC and MOON/LTC were both added to CoinEx, the first ever exchange to add the coin.

On the 6th of January 2014, it was added to Coinmarketcap.com. On the 23rd, a community Facebook group (www.facebook.com/MooncoinCurrency) was founded. Mooncoin reached an all time high of about $6,001,550 in terms of market cap on the 24th of January 2014. At this peak, one MOON was worth 0.00029 mBTC. Cryptsy added the trading pair MOON/LTC to their exchange one day earlier to this peak.

On the 20th of February, the new official website (http://mooncoin.info/) was created. On the 21st, Kimoto's Gravity Well was introduced into MOON via a hard fork in the blockchain at block number 26,850. With the help of http://multipool.us, the last few blocks were successfully mined and block 26,850 was reached sooner rather than later. Wallet users had to download and install the new wallet version preferably before the update occurred in order to continue on the correct blockchain.

In the middle of March, the MOON/BTC trading pair was removed from Cryptsy.

On the 3rd of April, the Mooncoin source code was updated to address KGW vulnerability. The Windows wallet was released the same day and the Mac OS X wallet the following day courtesy of "Forum Superstar Mac-jockey Maxpower".

On the 20th of June, "deaconboogie" announced the intention of transferring the development of Mooncoin over to the community rather than him being the sole developer. He said he would still remain part of the team. A leadership group would be set up to direct the coin's future.

On the 1st of October, the Mooncoin wallet ceased to be in maintenance and offline. It was offline for a few weeks. On the 22nd of October, Mooncoin was added to CryptoShop, a site on which MOON can be purchased by using PayPal.

On the 21st of November, Mooncoin became the 5th most active coin on Cryptsy in terms of trade volume at about 28.4 BTC over a 24 hour period. Eight days earlier, it topped the Cryptsy LTC market trading pairs at a 10.6 BTC trading volume. In the month of November, the market cap of the coin more than tripled from the 10th to the 23rd of November 2014.

www.facebook.com/pages/Mooncoin/265733153576906
www.reddit.com/r/MoonCoin/
www.twitter.com/RealMooncoin

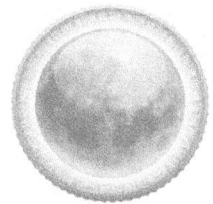

MISCELLANEOUS

There was a rumour in the community of a virus in the official wallet. This was unfounded as the wallet in question belonged to an individual who had created his own wallet with faulty code.

As the coin's name suggest, the community believe in its future potential as being a main competitor. To the Moon!

CoinEx added Mooncoin to its virtual currency trading floor within the coin's first 12 hours of existence, unprecedented for a crypto-currency launch.

The current Mooncoin coin logo was designed by "deaconboogie".

EXCHANGES

CoinEX (added on ~31/12/13)
Coined Up (added on ~03/01/14)
Cryptsy (added on ~23/01/14)
Cryptokk (added on ~04/04/14)
Swisscex (added on ~04/04/14)
AGX (added on ~04/05/14)
Cryptoine (added on ~31/05/14)
Bleutrade (added on ~29/09/14)

MOON TEAM

"deaconboogie"—Founder

MOON

NXT

"NEXT GENERATION OF CRYPTOCURRENCY"

Proof of Stake

NXT

NXT

"NEXT GENERATION OF CRYPTOCURRENCY"

SPECIFICATION

Symbol:	NXT
Launched:	24th of November 2013
Timestamping Algorithm:	Proof of Stake
Total Coins:	1 billion
Block Time/Difficulty Retarget:	1 minute/every block

- Nxt is described as a second generation cryptocurrency.

- It is based on new software code.

- It is not a fork of Bitcoin or other altcoins such as Litecoin or Peercoin.

- It cannot be mined using computational hardware.

- Addresses exist as strings of numbers of varying length.

- It was the first cryptocurrency to employ a 100% proof of stake algorithm.

- All one billion coins were initially available from the start. From day one, these coins are being distributed and dispersed to a growing number of users.

- Coins are rewarded entirely via transaction fees in the network.

- It implements a feature which allows rates of transactions to reach Visa/Mastercard levels. This is possible due to "Transparent Forging".

- The Nxt network is maintained by those who actually own NXT coins.

- It was the responsibility of the initial stakeholders to distribute NXT through the network via exchanges and online forums.

http://nxt.org/	(Official Website)
http://87.230.14.1/nxt/nxt.cgi?action=1	(Block Explorer)
https://nxtforum.org/	(Official Forum)
http://nxter.org/	(News Website)

NXT

HISTORY

"NEXT GENERATION OF CRYPTOCURRENCY"

NXT

Before launch, the crypto community were given 6 weeks notice. On the 28th of September 2013, "BCnext" created the Bitcointalk thread on which he asked for tiny donations of BTC to help fund Nxt. It was then their responsibility to distribute NXT through the network via exchanges and online forums. On the 19th of October, the stakeholders voted on which advanced features they would like to see developed next . "Coloured coins" was the winning feature.

On the 18th of November, after fundraising had ceased, 73 initial stakeholders had donated a total of about 21 BTC. Six days later, the genesis block was created. 1,000,000,000 coins were distributed to 73 stakeholders, with the proportion of coins received dependent upon each stakeholder's portion of the original fundraising total. Nxt's original market capitalization was $800,000USD. Nxt was listed on DGEX on the 28th of November. The community stated that the exchange is temporary due to it being centralised.

On the 4th of December, Nxt was added to the site Coinmarketcap.com. On the 20th, a client (V 0.4.0) was released. It enabled the ability to process alias requests from block number 22,000.

On the 1st of January 2014, a client (V 0.4.8) was released. This enabled transparent forging from block number 30,000. Two days later, the source code was released. On the 13th, a client (V 0.5.4e) was released. It enabled arbitrary messages from block number 40,000. Nxt reached an all time high of about $108,454,098 in terms of market cap on the 21st of January. At this peak, one NXT was worth 0.16504 mBTC according to Bter.

On the 1st of March, the source code was fully released.

On the 27th of April, a new Bitcointalk thread was created by "Damelon". One day later, the NRS (V 1.0.0) was released, including a new client interface.

On the 6th of May, account leasing was enabled from block number 130,000. A hard fork was introduced at this block and users had to upgrade. On the 12th, the asset exchange went live at block number 135,000. From the 21st, users have been able to send emails by using the Nxt blockchain. At the end of May, Nxt reached number three on Coinmarketcap at a cap of about $50,013,503.

On the 4th of June, "Daniella's Wacky Café" in Shoreham was the first cafe in the world to accept Nxt coin.

On the 20th of July, the Danish Bitcoin Exchange CCEDK was the first to launch a NXT to fiat gateway. Nine days later, the NXT decentralised exchange Multigateway" launched to the public.

On the 15th of August, about 51 million NXT (~3355.73 BTC or $1,701,015) were stolen from the Chinese exchange Bter. Bter took responsibility. As a result of the theft, the NXT community discussed whether or not to roll back the blockchain to erase the transactions. A majority of the community voted not to do it.

On the 13th of September, the Nxt Android app was released on Google Play.

On the 5th of October, the Nxt iPhone wallet app was released.

www.facebook.com/nxtcrypto
www.reddit.com/r/NXT/
www.twitter.com/NxtCrypto

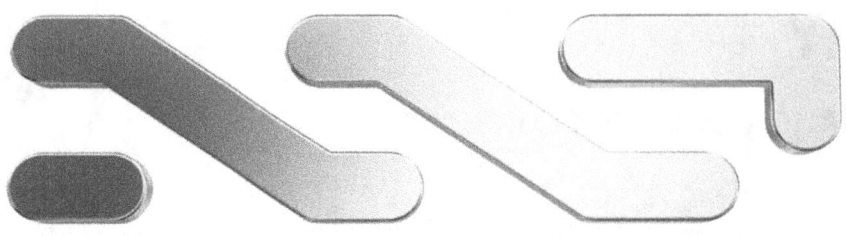

NXT GENERATION OF CRYPTOCURRENCY

MISCELLANEOUS

Nxt has the potential to allow further decentralised services such as peer-to-peer messaging, voting systems and coloured coins.

Nxt is developing a decentralised exchange on which only regular network transaction fees will apply.

The nxtQuant is to Nxt as a Satoshi is to Bitcoin.

The Nxt Asset Exchange generates NXT for forgers.

NXTlegal is a non-profit project to help Nxt users with legal issues.

NXTblocks is an online wallet for the Nxt cryptocurrency platform and an advanced block explorer for the NXT blockchain. It began on the 18th of May 2014 solely with the block explorer. The online wallet feature began on the 28th of June 2014.

EXCHANGES

DGEX (added on ~28/11/13)
Bter (added on ~18/01/14)
Poloniex (added on ~18/01/14)
Vircurex (added on ~27/01/14)
Cryptsy (added on ~02/03/14)
Bittrex (added on ~03/03/14)
BTC38 (added on ~08/03/14)
Crypto-Trade (added on ~12/06/14)
CCEDK (added on ~20/07/14)
HitBTC (added on ~08/08/14)
C-Cex (added on ~21/08/14)

NXT DEVELOPERS

Jean-Luc
Come-from-Beyond
kushti
jl777
ChuckOne

PEERCOIN

"The Secure & Sustainable Cryptocoin"

SHA-256 Hybrid PoW/PoS

BLOCK REWARD FORMULA

$$\left\{ \frac{9{,}999^{4}}{\text{DIFFICULTY}} \right\}^{1/4}$$

For each 16x increase in the network difficulty, the Proof of Work block reward is halved according to Moore's Law. Difficulty changes every block so sudden halving shocks are avoided. Initial difficulty was 256, so the reward at this time was approximately 2,500 coins.

The above formula calculates the coin reward of each block based on the difficulty of that block. So as the difficulty of mining the coins increases, the block reward decreases.

PPC

PEERCOIN

"The Secure & Sustainable Cryptocoin"
"New & Improved Bitcoin"

SPECIFICATION

Symbol:	PPC, ₽
Launched (Founders):	19th of August 2012 ("Sunny King"/Scott Nadal)
Hashing Algorithm:	SHA-256
Timestamping Algorithm:	Hybrid Proof of Work/Proof of Stake
Address Begins With:	P
Total Coins:	(see below)
Block Time/Difficulty Retarget:	10 minutes/10 minutes (1 block)
Coins per Block:	2,499.75 (initially)
Confirmations per Transaction:	6
Pre-mine:	None

- The first implementation of hybrid proof of work and proof of stake.

- Reward varies based on the difficulty per block. The initial difficulty for PoW mining was 256.

- Aims to achieve high energy-efficiency.

- Unlike Bitcoin, Peercoin does not require the use of energy to sustain the network.

- Until v0.2 of the client, central checkpointing was a critical part of the protocol. The main purpose of this was to defend the network (from double spending) during the growth period and to ensure a smooth upgrade path if any critical vulnerabilities were found. Central checkpointing will slowly be weakened and should eventually be removed from the coin.

- PPCoin only has a hard cap of 2 billion coin in the code (not expected to get close to this value).

- Forked from Bitcoin.

- Minimum age for coins used in a stake block is 30 days. A 1% annual return for held coins. The number of confirmations needed for proof of stake blocks is 520.

http://peercoin.net	(Official Website)
http://blockexplorer.ppcointalk.org/	(Block Explorer)
http://www.peercointalk.org/	(Official Forum)

PPC

HISTORY

"The Secure & Sustainable Cryptocoin"

"New & Improved Bitcoin"

The Peercoin Project began in October 2011. A new form of timestamping called proof of stake was independently discovered after studying Nakamoto's work. Peercoin was pre-announced by "Sunny King" on the 10th of August 2012 on Bitcointalk. Just before the launch of the coin, a Peercoin design paper, the first official website (www.peercoin.org) and the source code were released.

Peercoin launched on the 16th of August 2012 at 18:00 UTC. A new Bitcointalk thread was created by "Sunny King" slightly beforehand to coincide with this. On the 26th, the first Peercoin forum (www.peercointalk.org) was created thanks to "FuzzyBear". Also in August, a client (V 0.2) was released. It made it possible for wallet users to see the total number of Peercoin currently in circulation.

On the 4th of September, the first exchange to add Peercoin was CryptoCoin thanks to "mugen". On the 18th, the first block explorer (http://www.ppcexplore.org:2750) was made by "dreamwatcher". Also on the 18th, the first proof of stake block was generated.

On the 3rd of October, the total number of Peercoin in circulation surpassed 10 million. On the 15th, the Peercoin blockchain passed block number 10,000 (10:41:39 UTC).

In early December, the first Peercoin payment processor (cryptocoinsend) was created thanks to "xchrix".

On the 18th of February 2013, after many weeks of testing, a client (V 0.3.0) was released. It improved many aspects of the proof of stake timestamping algorithm. Users had to install the new client before the 20th of March 2013 because of the scheduled future hard fork. Thanks were made to "dreamwatcher", "Jatarul" and "EskimoBob". Also in February, the first Peercoin fork called Novacoin was launched.

On the 22nd of May, Peercoin became available for tipping on Reddit.

On the 11th of July, after many rounds of voting, logo #199 (current coin logo) won the logo coin contest.

On the 18th of October, the official Facebook group was founded. On the 30th, the official website was redesigned and the first Peercoin newsletter was published.

On the 4th of November, the official Twitter page was founded. On the 6th, the market cap surpassed $10 million for the first time. On the 18th, the value of one Peercoin reached $1. Peercoin reached an all time high of about £185,313,050 in terms of market cap on the 30th of November. At this peak, one PPC was worth 0.00796 BTC according to BTC-e.

On the 6th of April 2014, a client (V 0.4) was released. This client had to be installed before the 4th of May 2014, one day in advance of a hard fork.

On the 2nd of June, Peerunity 0.1.0, a community-developed wallet client, was released.

On the 19th of July, a new Peercoin promotional video was made public on YouTube.

On the 8th of September, the official Peercoin website was newly designed.

https://www.facebook.com/Peercoin
http://www.reddit.com/r/peercoin
https://twitter.com/PeercoinPPC

MISCELLANEOUS

It was the first cryptocurrency to use proof of stake as part of its timestamping algorithm.

SatoshiRoulette.com was the first to accept PPC as payment.

"Sunny King" gets involved in helping other developers with other coins. He sees the cryptocurrency community working towards a common goal.

The main goal of Peercoin is to show that energy efficiency in the cryptocurrency space is successful.

Direct Voltage (directvoltage.com) was the first retailer to accept PPC as payment on the 29th of April 2013.

The logo design project of the current coin logo was lead by "Sentinelrv".

Peerunity, Peershares, Peerbox and NuBits are current Peercoin community projects under development.

EXCHANGES

CryptoCoin (added on ~04/09/12)
Bitparking (added on ~07/09/12)
Vircurex (added on ~19/11/12)
BTC-e (added on ~06/04/13)
Bter (added on ~24/04/13)
Cyptsy (added on ~23/05/13)
Crypto Trade (added on ~10/06/13)
Coins-e (added on ~15/07/13)
mcxNOW (added on ~29/09/13)
CoinEX (added on ~30/09/13)
Vault of Satoshi (added on ~28/10/13)
C-Cex (added on ~16/01/14)
Bittylicious (added on ~30/01/14)
Bittrex (added on ~28/02/14)
Poloniex (added on ~08/04/14)
CCEDK (added on ~23/09/14)

PPC TEAM

Sunny King—Core Development
Sigmike—Core Development
Sentinelrv—Social Media
Kappamale—Subreddit Administrator
FuzzyBear—Peercointalk Administrator

Cybnate—Marketing Fund
River333—Marketing Fund
Super3—Peercoin.net Web Developer
TheWildHorse—Peercoin.net Web Developer
Chronos—Peercoin.net Web Developer

PPC

PRIMECOIN

"THE FIRST SCIENTIFIC COMPUTING CRYPTOCURRENCY"

Cunningham Proof of Work

BLOCK REWARD FORMULA

$$\left\{ \frac{999}{DIFFICULTY^2} \right\}$$

The above formula calculates the coin reward of each block based on the difficulty of that block. So as the difficulty of mining the coins increases, the block reward decreases.

XPM

PRIMECOIN

"THE FIRST SCIENTIFIC COMPUTING CRYPTOCURRENCY"

SPECIFICATION

Symbol:	XPM, Ψ
Launched (Founder):	7th of July 2013 ("Sunny King")
Hashing Algorithm:	Cunningham
Timestamping Algorithm:	Proof of Work
Address Begins With:	A
Total Coins:	25 million
Block Time/Difficulty Retarget:	1 minute/every block
Coins per Block:	(see below)
Confirmations per Transaction:	6
Pre-mine:	None

- It is the first cryptocurrency on the market with non-hashcash proof-of-work, generating additional potential scientific value from mining work . It uses a prime PoW algorithm which generates special chains of prime numbers. It has served to further mathematical research into prime numbers.

- Difficulty is smoothly adjusted every block based on previous block hashrates .

- Initial difficulty was 7. This equated to an initial block reward of about 20.39 XPM.

- A maximum estimated coin supply of 25 million.

- Number of coins rewarded per block is 999 divided by the square of the difficulty (Moore's Law). As the difficulty of the network increases, the block rewards will decrease accordingly.

- The Primecoin source code is copyrighted by a person or a group called the "Primecoin Developers", and distributed under a conditional MIT/X11.

- The currency symbol Ψ was chosen as a tribute Riemann, the influential German mathematician.

http://primecoin.io/	(Official Website)
https://coinplorer.com/XPM	(Block Explorer)
http://www.peercointalk.org/	(Official Forum)

XPM

HISTORY

"THE FIRST SCIENTIFIC COMPUTING CRYPTOCURRENCY"

The Primecoin project was conceived in March 2013.

On the 28th of June, a pre-release Bitcointalk forum thread was created by "Sunny King" in order to announce the final beta stages of Primecoin development. Towards the end of this thread, the launch time was scheduled at 18:00 UTC on the 7th of July 2013.

On the 7th of July 2013, just before the launch time, a new Bitcointalk thread was created and the Peercoin design paper was made public. This paper details the reasons why primes have been incorporated into the code. This document is titled "Primecoin: Cryptocurrency with Prime Number Proof of Work". The official forum was already active. It shares the same forum as Peercoin (http://www.peercointalk.org/). Also on the same day, the first block explorer was created thanks to "ahmed_bodi". On the 10th, the official Twitter page was founded and it was added to the site www.coinmarketcap.com. On the 19th, the total daily trading volume over four exchanges passed over 2,000 BTC. On the 25th, the official Facebook group was created.

In August, a client (V 0.1.2) is released and "mikaelh" joined the Primecoin development team.

Primecoin reached an all time high of about \$24,775,226 in terms of market cap on the 30th of November 2013. At this peak, one XPM was worth 0.0066 BTC according to BTC-e. At the end of November, BTC-e added the trading pair XPM/USD to their exchange.

In January 2014, Primecoin reached a new record for 13-primes, a 107 digit Cunningham chain of first kind.

In February, a client (hp12) was released thanks to "Mikael". This client was described as possessing high performance compared with the usual clients. Also, the Primecoin official website (www.primecoin.io) was previewed thanks to "Super3".

On the 29th of March 2014, use first GPU miner for mining Primecoin became publicly available. An increase in the network difficulty close to 11 understandably occurred before this happened.

On the 16th of May, the first 14 length Cunningham chain of the second kind was found.

In early June 2014, the Primecoin network reached another milestone by discovering a 14-prime chain at block number 547,276, a Cunningham chain of 2nd kind with 100 digits.

On the 21st of July 2014, "Sunny King" was interviewed by Sean Mikha (Let's Talk Bitcoin). He was questioned over the fact that he continues to keep his real identity secret, despite Charlie Lee of Litecoin revealing his true self one year earlier. Also in July, Primecoin had achieved 5 out of a total of 21 world records in simultaneous prime numbers.

On the 18th of September, Primecoin was added to pock.io (users can buy giftcards with cryptocurrency).

On the 10th of December, an article was written by www.investopedia.com titled "The 5 Most Important Virtual Currencies Other Than Bitcoin". At the time, the market cap of Primecoin was \$961,543.

www.facebook.com/PrimecoinXPM
www.reddit.com/r/primecoin
www.twitter.com/Primecoin

MISCELLANEOUS

Primecoin has been one of the four mayor denominations along with BTC, LTC and DOGE on certain exchanges as trading pairs (XPM can be traded directly with many other coins).

Primecoin is innovative and unique in the sense that it has its own cryptogenic algorithm and incorporates Moore's Law into its calculations.

World records for finding Cunningham chains of varying lengths are found on a regular basis.

The first world record claimed by Primecoin was on the 8th of July 2013. This was at block 2,044 with the new world record for 2CC09 (131).

Satoshi Roulette was the first service to accept Primecoin as a form of payment.

"Sunny King" is clear in saying that Peercoin is more important than Primecoin in the long term.

EXCHANGES

Coins-e (added on ~10/07/13)
mcxNOW (added on ~11/07/13)
Vircurex (added on ~11/07/13)
Cryptsy (added on ~12/07/13)
Crypto-Trade (added on ~20/07/13)
Bter (added on ~02/09/13)
BTC-e (added on ~13/10/13)
Coined Up (added on ~25/11/13)
Poloniex (added on ~16/02/14)

XPM TEAM

Sunny King—Core Development
Sigmike—Core Development
Sentinelrv—Social Media
Kappamale—Subreddit Administrator
FuzzyBear—Primecointalk Administrator

Cybnate—Marketing Fund
River333—Marketing Fund
mikaelh—Developer

XPM

QUARK

"MONEY REINVENTED"

SHA-3 Proof of Work

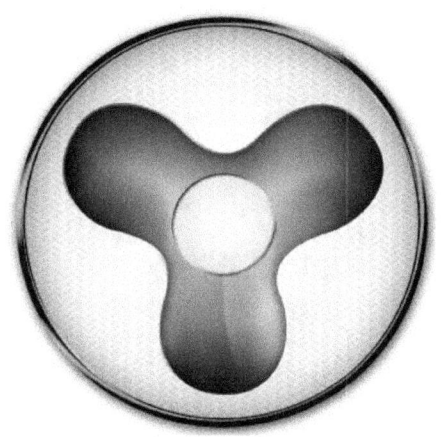

BLOCK REWARD DISTRIBUTION SCHEDULE TABLE

Block Phase	Block Number	Reward	Date of Initial Block
Initial Phase	1-60,479	2048	~21st of July 2013
1st Halving	60,480-120,959	1024	~10th of August 2013
2nd Halving	120,960-181,439	512	~31st of August 2013
3rd Halving	181,440-241,919	256	~20th of September 2013
4th Halving	241,920-302,399	128	~10th of October 2013
————————	————————	————————	————————————
8th Halving	483,840-544,319	8	~24th of December 2013
9th Halving	544,320-604,799	4	~13th January 2014
10th Halving	604,800-665,279	2	~2nd of February 2014
Fixed Phase	665,280————	1	~23rd of February 2014

QRK

QUARK

"QUARK IS THE NEXT GENERATION CRYPTOCURRENCY"
"MONEY REINVENTED"

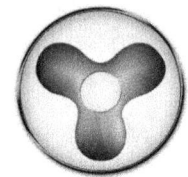

SPECIFICATION

Symbol:	QRK
Launched (Founder):	21st of July 2013 (Max Guevara)
Hashing Algorithm:	SHA-3 (blake, groestl, blue midnight wish, jh, SHA-3, skein)
Timestamping Algorithm:	Proof of Work
Address Begins With:	Q
Total Coins:	247 million (+ ~1 million QRK per year thereafter)
Block Time/Difficulty Retarget:	30 seconds/every 20 blocks (10 minutes)
Coins per Block:	(see the first page)
Confirmations per Transaction:	5
Pre-mine:	None

♦ Protected by 9 rounds of hashing from 6 different hash functions. It gives Quark an extra layer of security that makes it less susceptible to future attack. Three rounds apply a random hashing function.

♦ Mined by regular PC power (CPU) but not by ASICs. Quark is ASIC proof due to the six hashing functions. It would be very costly to mine Quark with ASICs.

♦ Quark's initial mining has produced a total of 247 million Quark (5-6 months). Each year about one million Quark are released through mining. This means that Quark is uncapped with a gradual rate of inflation of about 0.5% per year.

♦ Difficulty retargets every 20 blocks (maximum 10% up or 50% down)

♦ Quark also has the distinction of being one of the most-mined coins, as 548,325 blocks were created in just over six months. This was most likely done in order to quickly surpass the period of coin expansion.

http://qrk.cc (Official Website)
http://quarkexplorer.com (Information, transactions & blocks)
http://forum.qrk.cc/ (Official Forum)
http://www.quarkfoundation.cc/ (Foundation Website)
http://quarkuniverse.cc/

QRK

HISTORY

"QUARK IS THE NEXT GENERATION CRYPTOCURRENCY"

"MONEY REINVENTED"

QRK

On the 21st of July 2013, a developer who goes by the name of "Max Guevara" introduced this new cryptocurrency.

In August, the currently used Quark coin logo was designed by "ohiwastedmylif" and the first block explorer was launched thanks to "Abe". On the 25th of August, it was added to the site Coinmarketcap.com.

On the 28th of November, the Guardian mentioned Quark as one of nine Bitcoin alternatives.

In December 2013, Quark or "QuarkCoin" gained publicity from two mainstream commentators called Bill Still and Max Keiser on the news channel RT. Quark reached an all time high of about $71,017,813 in terms of market cap on the 2nd of December. At this peak, one QRK was worth 0.30997 mBTC according to Cryptsy. On the 4th, the Wall Street Journal wrote about the value of Quark increasing approximately 500% in the space of one week and topping the Cryptsy volume chart of all their listed coins. On the 5th, the Facebook group was launched.

On the 2nd of January 2014, the website www.quarkfoundation.com (forums and projects) was launched. On the 8th, the new official website (www.qrk.cc) was launched. On the 27th, a new block explorer was created at www.blockr.io

On the 9th of March, the beta Quark Android wallet became available on Google Play. On the 30th, the trading pair QRK/USD was added to Prelude

In April, Quark partnered with Moolah to provide fast and secure in-store and online payment solutions. In the same month, Quark also partnered with the Shaq-Fu 2 Team.

In early May, Big Deez Productions and the team behind "Shaq-Fu: A Legend Reborn" successfully raised $473,884 in donations. They exceeded their initial target of $450,000. On the 13th of May, altoutlet.com added Quark as a payment option on their website.

On the 8th of June, the Quark Foundation and community met with Max and Dam, the core developers. Two days later, Facebook officially approved a multi-coin tipping app, which includes Quark. The application was created by Alejandro Caballero. On the 29th of June, the Quark Android wallet was fully released (not beta) on Google Play thanks to user "Hash Engineering".

On the 25th of October, a client (V 0.9.2.1) was released. On the 30th, a video was posted on YouTube in which Shaquille O'neal endorses Quark.

www.facebook.com/quark.currency
www.reddit.com/r/QuarkCoin/
www.twitter.com/Quark_QRK

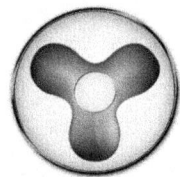

MISCELLANEOUS

Max Guevara is involved in keeping the coin and network healthy by releasing regular checkpoints.

The foundation was created by members of the Quark community. The foundation currently has nine members who each look after current and future projects related of the coin.

EXCHANGES

Coins-e (added on ~22/07/13)
Cryptsy (added on ~25/07/13)
Bter (added on ~31/08/13)
PhenixEx (added on ~04/09/13)
Vircurex (added on ~15/12/13)
BTC-8 (added on ~02/01/14)
CoinedUp (added on ~11/01/14)
BCT38 (added on ~19/01/14)
Coin-Swap (added on ~29/01/14)
Swisscex (added on ~02/02/14)
Cryptokopen (added on ~03/02/14)
Litebit (added on ~06/02/14)
C-Cex (added on ~11/02/14)
Bittylicious (added on ~15/02/14)
Bleutrade (added on ~25/03/14)
Moolah (added on ~30/03/14)
Vault of Sat (added on ~02/04/14)
Bittrex (added on ~26/04/14)
QEX (added on ~25/05/14)

QRK TEAM

James Z—Webmaster (Official Website and QF)
Victor—PR (writes press releases for www.qrk.cc)
Penny—PR of the Quark Foundation (QF)
Max Guevara—Head Developer

Adam—QRK wallet developer
Matrixfighter—PR (Reddit Page)

QRK

REDDCOIN

"THE SOCIAL CURRENCY"

Scrypt Proof of Stake Velocity (PoSV)

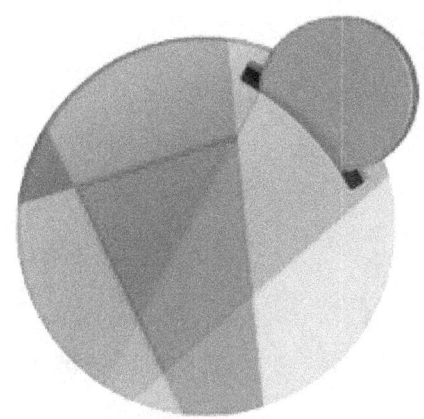

BLOCK REWARD DISTRIBUTION SCHEDULE TABLE

Block Phase	Block Number	Reward	Date of Initial Block
IPCO Pre-mine	1-10	545,000,000	~26th of January 2014
Bonus 1	11-9,999	300,000	~2nd of February 2014
Bonus 2	10,000-19,999	200,000	~9th of February 2014
Bonus 3	20,000-29,999	150,000	~16th of February 2014
Fifth Phase	30,000-139,999	100,000	~23rd of February 2014
1st Halving	140,000-189,999	50,000	~10th of May 2014
2nd Halving	190,000-239,999	25,000	~14th of June 2014
3rd Halving	240,000-260,799	12,500	~19th of July 2014
PoSV Phase	260,800—————		~2nd of August 2014

Reddcoin is now entirely generated by staking coins in a user's wallet client.

RDD

REDDCOIN

"THE SOCIAL CURRENCY"

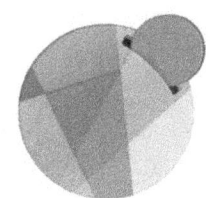

SPECIFICATION

Symbol:	RDD, R
Launched (Founders):	2nd of February 2014 ("Laudney" and "Reddcoin")
Hashing Algorithm:	Scrypt
Timestamping Algorithm:	Proof of Stake Velocity (PoSV)
Address Begins With:	R
Total coins:	~27 billion (+ 5% maximum annual inflation)
Block Time/Difficulty Retarget:	60 seconds/60 seconds (KGW)
Coins per Block:	(see the first page)
Confirmations per Transaction:	6
Pre-mine:	5%

- Difficulty retargets every block using Kimoto's Gravity Well.

- The number of coins was approximately just short of 27 billion at the end of proof of work.
  The number of coins reached 27 billion on the 12th of September 2014.

- A maximum 5% yearly inflation due to a new algorithm called Proof of Stake Velocity (PoSV). PoSV is an innovative algorithm that encourages both ownership (stake) and activity (velocity).

- The total number of coins available in the IPCO was 5.45 billion, which were released to investors on a daily basis for 90 days from the 16th of February 2014. (1.11% of the total received was distributed to each investor each day, ending in mid-May 2014).

- The original coin total was 109 billion coins and it was a clone of Litecoin (Originally based on the Litecoin v0.8.6.2 source code). It was intended that after 500,000 blocks the reward for generating a block decreased by 50%. However, the block reward scheme was changed before this was reached.

- Users are able to mint/stake coins in their own wallet clients at an annual interest of 5%.

http://reddcoin.com	(Official Website)
http://bitinfocharts.com/reddcoin/explorer/	(Block Explorer)
http://reddcoinforum.com/	(Official Forum)
http://reddheads.com/	(News Platform)
http://wesellredd.com/	(Buy Reddcoin)

RDD

HISTORY

"THE SOCIAL CURRENCY"

On the 20th of January 2014, Reddcoin was announced on Bitcointalk by user "Reddcoin" as a Scrypt proof of work coin. Prior to its launch, a successful initial public coin offering occurred. This raised funds to expand Reddcoin's network and infrastructure. A total of 386 investors pledged about 168.83 BTC during Reddcoin's IPCO. On the 30th, "Ricky0819" was the first member of the Reddcoin team hired by "Reddcoin".

Stage one of the IPCO finished on the 2nd of February, just before the launch (55.32399750 BTC pledged from 245 investors). On the same day, the Windows client (V 10) and the source code were released. A block explorer was also created on the same day thanks to "candidakefyr" as well as the Facebook group. On the 3rd, Reddcoin was added to Coin Market as the RDD/BTC trading pair and Fresh Market as RDD/LTC. On the 6th, the wallet client (V 1.1) was released in order to fix issues with multi-pools. From block 6,000, new settings similar to Megacoin and Vertcoin initiated. On the 9th, it was added to Coinmarketcap.com. On the 15th the IPCO stage ended and a new coin logo was chosen after three rounds of voting. Two days later, the wallet client (V 1.1.1) was released. On the 25th, the Reddcoin tipbot went live on Twitter.

On the 6th of March, a wallet client (V 1.1.3) was released. Reddcoin reached an all time high one day later at about $1,126,147 in terms of market cap. At this peak, one RDD was worth 0.00014 mBTC according to Coined Up. Reddcoin experienced its first test of resilience on the 9th when a flaw in the source code was exploited and the Reddcoin network was temporarily taken offline. Within 24 hours the source code was repaired and the network was restored. On the 13th, the RDD Android app became available on Google Play. On the 15th, /r/Reddcoin had become the fourth largest cryptocurrency community on Reddit.

On the 5th of April, the official ReddAPI was launched. It is designed to enable easy interfacing between Reddcoin and developer projects. On the 10th, users had to update to client wallet (V 1.1.3.2). It fixed problems caused by the Heartbleed Bug. On the 13th, the "Reddcoin Broadcast" went live. On the 29th, it was announced that Reddcoin would transition to a brand new proof of stake velocity (PoSV) algorithm.

On the 1st of May, a mandatory client (V 1.2.0.0) was released. On the 10th, the block reward of Reddcoin halved from 100,000 to 50,000 coins. The community had a block halving party to celebrate this milestone.

On the 20th of July, Cryptsy added the trading pair RDD/USD. On the 23rd, the PoSV wallet client (V 1.3.0.0) was released. This was a mandatory update. On the 26th, one RDD reached the same value as one DOGE at 35 Satoshi. Reddcoin reached a new all time high of about $6,373,318 in terms of market cap on the 27th. At this peak, one RDD was worth 0.0004 mBTC according to Cryptsy.

On the 2nd of August, proof of stake velocity (PoSV) began at block 260,800.

On the 6th of September, lead developer Larry Ren announced phase 2 of Reddcoin development, Social X.

On the 3rd of October, the official block explorer (http://live.reddcoin.com/) was released. On the 8th, the first Reddcoin newsletter was published.

On the 2nd of December, a YouTube video showing a quick demonstration of the upcoming browser wallet was published.

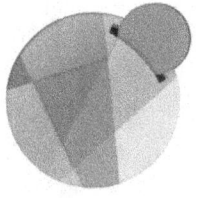

www.facebook.com/reddcoin
www.reddit.com/r/reddCoin/
www.twitter.com/reddcoin

The original logo used initially until the current was chosen.

On the 15th of February, the current RDD logo won first prize in a poll. This logo got 120 ratings, an average rating of 4 with 64 ratings of star 5/5 in the penultimate poll. Logo was designed by user "Alexandark"

MISCELLANEOUS

Reddcoin is marketed as a social currency. Its developers are in the process of integrating RDD with all major social networks.

The ultimate intention of RDD is for tipping on social networks, much like Fedoracoin, and serves as a way to increase the awareness of cryptocurrency to the general public through social media.

Reddcoin have a tip platform and a broadcast platform.

The IPCO existed in order to create enough money to invest in the project. The sum of stage one was 2,200,000,021 RDD and the sum of stage two was 3,249,999,000 RDD.

Reddcoin is in reference to the social platform Reddit, unlike Redcoin which is in reference to the colour red.

EXCHANGES

Coinmarket (added on ~03/02/14)
Freshmarket (added on ~03/02/14)
CryptX (added on ~09/02/14)
Cryptorush (added on ~20/02/14)
Poloniex (added on ~24/02/14)
Bittrex (added on ~25/02/14)
Coined Up (added on ~06/03/14)
Cryptsy (added on ~14/03/14)
AGX (added on ~20/03/14)
Coin Swap (added on ~22/03/14)
Swisscex (added on ~06/04/14)
AllCrypt (added on ~20/04/14)
Prelude (added on ~22/04/14)
Coin Next (added on ~22/05/14)
MintPal (added on ~18/07/14)
Allcoin (added on ~29/07/14)

RDD TEAM

Laudney (UK)—Leader Developer, Co-founder
Reddcoin (Canada) - Developer, Co-founder
MathyV (Belgium) - Developer
lionzeye (Netherlands) - Developer
Andrew (USA/Turkey) - Developer

raid5 (USA) - Developer
ezredd (USA/France) - Contributor
reddibrek (Belgium) - Reddheads.com Editor
bigreddmachine (USA) - wiki.reddcoin.com Editor

RDD

SATURN2COIN

"LET'S GET READY FOR THE FIRST FLIGHT TO SATURN!"

Scrypt Proof of Stake

BLOCK REWARD DISTRIBUTION SCHEDULE TABLE

Block Phase	Block Number	Reward	Date of Initial Block
Initial Phase	1	7,777,777	~28th of June 2014
Second Phase	2-200	0.1	~28th of June 2014
Third Phase	201-7,560	10	~28th of June 2014
1st Halving	7,561-15,120	5	~5th of July 2014
2nd Halving	15,121-21,600	2.5	~12th of July 2014

Proof of work mining ceased at block number 21,600.
Saturn2coin is now solely a proof of stake coin.

The initial number of SAT2 was 7.7 million.

SAT2

SATURN2COIN

"LET'S GET READY FOR THE FIRST FLIGHT TO SATURN!"
"FAST—FUN—SECURE"

SPECIFICATION

Symbol:	SAT2
Launched (Founder):	28th of June 2014 ("saturncoins")
Hashing Algorithm:	Scrypt
Timestamping Algorithm:	Proof of Stake
Address Begins With:	S
Total Coins:	(see below)
Block Time/Difficulty Retarget:	20 seconds/KGW
Coins per Block:	(see below)
Confirmations per Transaction:	Unknown
Pre-mine:	None

♦ The original coin, Saturncoin, was solely proof of work. It was launched on the 1st of February 2014.

♦ All SAT were automatically converted to SAT2 in time for the launch of SAT2 on exchanges.

♦ The initial number of SAT2 was 7.7 million. A total of 7.7 billion SAT were converted SAT2.

♦ Upto block number 21,600, the associated block time for proof of work mining was 80 seconds.

♦ Proof of stake annual interest is 10% for the first year, 5% for the second and 2.5% for the third year.

♦ Minimum coin age is ten days for staking.

♦ Maximum coin age is twenty days for staking.

♦ 1% of all staked/minted coins go towards a development fund.

http://saturn2.co.in/   (Official Website)   **SAT2**

HISTORY

"LET'S GET READY FOR THE FIRST FLIGHT TO SATURN!"

"FAST—FUN—SECURE"

SAT2

User "saturncoin" launched the original Bitcointalk thread for SAT on the 31st of January 2014.

Saturncoin was initially listed on Cryptorush on the 1st of February.

At the beginning of March, Saturncoin reached number one position of those coins to be added to MintPal with 67,000 votes. On the 10th, the Saturncoin Facebook group was launched. A day later, the website Coinmarketcap.com listed it. Saturncoin reached an all time high of about $306,258 in terms of market cap on the 14th. At this peak, one SAT was worth 0.00499 mBTC. At the end of March, the Saturncoin Foundation was set up.

On the 3rd of April, a new Bitcointalk thread was created by "saturncoins". On the 16th, Funboxfilm, the developers of a new application called MovieJump, started to accept Bitcoin, Litecoin and chose Saturncoin as the 3rd accepted Cryptocurrency. Also in April, the foundation began to support three causes. These are "Protect Sumatra's Rainforest", "Stop Exploiting Cild Labourers" and "Help Save the Serengeti Centre in Tanzania".

On the 1st of May, an announcement on the SAT2 Bitcointalk thread was made. It detailed how the developers planned to transition to a brand new proof of stake blockchain. It was clear that changing the timestamping algorithm from solely proof of work to proof of stake would be troublesome. Also on the day, a client was released which implemented a new coin limit of 7.7 billion. On the 11th, a client was released which addressed problems related to a fork in the blockchain and changed the difficulty retarget algorithm to KGW. Some multipools did not update to this client version. On the 17th, the difficulty retarget algorithm changed to KGW.

On the 4th of June, a new official website (www.saturn2.co.in) was created ready for the transition to the new SAT2 blockchain. On the 28th, the SAT2 blockchain went live.

On the 1st of July, Mintpal had successfully converted all SAT to SAT2 on their exchange. All other exchanges followed on from this. Individuals with SAT on their own personal wallet clients were given the chance to swap 1,000 SAT for 1 SAT2 too. The last chance to swap was on the 13th of July.

From August 2014 to the present day, there has been very little evidence of coin development.

www.facebook.com/saturncoin
www.reddit.com/r/saturncoin/
www.twitter.com/Saturncoins

OLD SATURNCOIN SPECIFICATION

Symbol:	SAT
Algorithm:	Scrypt Proof of Work
Total Coins:	15 billion
Block Time/Difficulty Re-target:	80 seconds/KGW
Confirmations per Transaction:	4
Pre-mine:	1%

Initiallly the coins rewarded per block were random at 1-250,000. This reward halved every 30,000 blocks. On the first day, the block reward payment was x2. On the second day, the block reward payment was x1.5. There was a 1% possibility of the block reward being twice as much.

The Original Saturncoin Logo

MISCELLANEOUS

In the case of Saturncoin, there was initial confusion about the total limit of coin supply of either 15 or 50 billion. 15 billion was the correct figure.

"bitcoin-newbie" and "heisenburg" helped to design and implement the saturncoinfoundation.org site.

"Saturn has been known as the Greater Sun and its enigmas have amazed the scientific community for centuries, now it's time to bring Saturn in to the Cryptocurrency World."

The main reason why proof of work (Saurn2coin) lasted for a short period of time was to bridge the gap between the launch and the beginning of proof of stake minting. This kept the network functioning properly.

EXCHANGES

SAT EXCHANGES

Cryptorush (added on ~01/02/14)
Comkort (added on ~02/03/14)
Mintpal (added on ~03/03/14)
Coinader (added on ~04/03/14)
Cryptsy (added on ~14/03/14)
Allcrypt (added on ~17/04/14)

SAT2 EXCHANGES

Bittrex (added on ~29/06/14)

SAT2 TEAM

"saturncoins"—Founder

SAT2

TAGCOIN

"THE WORLD'S FIRST REWARDS CURRENCY"

Scrypt PoW/PoS Hybrid

BLOCK REWARD DISTRIBUTION SCHEDULE TABLE

Block Phase	Block Number	Reward	Date of Initial Block
Pre-mine	1-357	30	~26th of October 2013
Initial Phase	358-32,760	30	~27th of October 2013
1st 1% decrease	32,761-65,520	29.7	~27th of January 2014
2nd 1% decrease	65,521-98,280	29.403	~27th of April 2014
3rd 1% decrease	98,281-131,040	29.10897	~27th of July 2014

The block reward reduces by 1% approximately every three months.

TAG

TAGCOIN

"THE WORLD'S FIRST REWARDS CURRENCY"

SPECIFICATION

Symbol:	TAG
Launched/Founder:	27th of October 2013 ("tagbond")
Hashing Algorithm:	Scrypt
Timestamping Algorithm:	Proof of Work/Proof of Stake
Address Begins With:	T
Total Coins:	~100 million
Block Time/Difficulty Retarget:	4 minutes/2 hours (30 blocks)
Coins per Block:	30 (initially)
Confirmations per Transaction:	5
Pre-mine:	Yes (10,710 TAG)

- It is a proof of work/proof of stake hybrid cryptocurrency. As soon as the coins in someone's TAG wallet are 30 days old, 5% yearly interest applies. Proof of stake blocks are generated after 30 days of coin age.

- Proof of work subsidy reduces by 1% every 3 months, minimum reward of 3 coins.

- It uses the same difficulty re-target algorithm as Peercoin.

- A maximum creation limit of about 10,000 coins per day is in place.

- Tagcoin had a starting difficulty of 0.5.

http://tagcoin.org/   (Official Website)
http://explorer.tagcoin.org/   (Block Explorer)

TAG

HISTORY

"THE WORLD'S FIRST REWARDS CURRENCY"

TAG

Tagcoin was announced on Bitcointalk on the 24th of October 2013 by user "tagbond". His original plan in February 2013 was to create a centralised rewards currency before he learnt more about cryptocurrency.

Tagcoin was intially listed on CoinEx on the 28th of October 2013. On the same day, the Tagcoin Facebook group was founded and "tagbond" announced that all 10,710 TAG pre-mined will be given out over the next few weeks. On the 29th, a Windows client (V 1.01) was released. This was mandatory as it fixed wallet synchronisation issues and introduced checkpoints. One day later, thanks to "maxpower", the MAC OS X wallet was created. On the last day of October, the TAG personal cash wallet was released on Android

On the 5th of November, TAG was added to the site Coinmarketcap.com. On the 7th, the beta TagBond site (a trading platform) was up and running. One Tagcoin reached a value of $1 on the 25th of November 2013. Two days later the official website (www.tagcoin.org) was launched.

On the 28th of November, a bug was identified in the difficulty retargeting algorithm when proof of stake began. The first proof of stake block was generated at block 8,452. As a result, a hard fork was introduced to resolve this. Therefore, users had to upgrade to a new client (V 1.0.2) that changed the difficulty retargeting algorithm to that of Peercoin's and altered the transaction fees. The hard fork occurred at block 12,000.

Tagcoin reached an all time high of about $1,533,041 in terms of market cap on the 11th of January 2014. At this peak, one TAG was worth 0.0027 BTC according to Cryptsy. On the 19th, a mandatory updated client (V 1.0.3) was made available for download. It had to downloaded before the 2nd of February in order to fix the stake reward.

On the 5th of February, another client (V 1.0.4) was released (highly recommended) followed by another client (V 1.0.5) (mandatory).

In March, there was mistrust between "tagbond" and "ny2cafuse".

From April 2014 to the present day, there has been very little evidence of coin development.

www.twitter.com/TagCoin
www.facebook.com/tagcoin

MISCELLANEOUS

Tagcoins are used on the online community based platform called TAGBOND. It shares many characteristics with Facebook, Paypal and Google.   On the site, one can search and share Tagverts which are effectively promotions, advertisements or prizes.   Tagcoins are then rewarded to those who use the system.

Tagcoins are not restricted solely to TAGBOND.

By combining rewards with the currency, Tagcoin generates engagement between potential buyers and sellers.

EXCHANGES

CoinEx (added on ~28/10/13)
Bter (added on ~29/10/13)
Cryptsy (added on ~31/10/13)
BTC38 (added on ~28/11/13)

TAG TEAM

"tagbond"—Founder

TAG

TOPCOIN2

"TO THE TOP!"

Scrypt PoW/PoS Hybrid

BLOCK REWARD DISTRIBUTION SCHEDULE TABLE

Block Phase	Block Number	Reward	Date of Initial Block
Initial Phase	1-525,599	5	~3rd of September 2014
1st Halving	525,600-1,051,199	2.5	~3rd of September 2017
2nd Halving	1,051,200-1,576,799	1.25	~3rd of September 2020
3rd Halving	1,576,800-2,102,399	0.625	~3rd of September 2023

And so on...

The block reward halves approximately every 3 years.

TOP2

TOPCOIN2

"TO THE TOP!"

SPECIFICATION

Symbol:	TOP2
Launched (Founder):	3rd of September 2014 ("topdude")
Hashing Algorithm:	Scrypt
Timestamping Algorithm:	Hybrid Proof of Work/Proof of Stake
Address Begins With:	T
Total Coins:	No hard limit
Block Time/Difficulty Retarget:	60 seconds/every block
Coins per Block:	(see the first page)
Confirmations per Transactions:	4
Pre-mine:	None

♦ Topcoin was initially solely a Scrypt proof of work coin.

♦ Topcoin2 proof of work is initially 5 coins per block. This reward halves every 3 years.

♦ Topcoin2 proof of stake is 50% annually. This is paid to wallet users daily.

♦ There is a weekly 0.1% PoS interest rate on coins held in a user's wallet.

♦ Please see the top of page 168 for further details of the original Topcoin specification.

http://topcoin.pw/ (Official Website)
http://blocks.topcoin.pw/ (Block Explorer)

TOP2

HISTORY

"TO THE TOP!"

On the 2nd of February, Topcoin was announced on Bitcointalk by user "topdude". On the same day, the Topcoin blockchain went live.

On the 10th of February, the official Twitter page was created. On the 11th, "crymzyn" announced the Mount Everest project fundraiser. On the 12th, the official website was created (www.topcoin.pw) and a client (V 1.2) was released. On the 16th, Topcoin was added to the site Coinmarketcap.com. Topcoin reached an all time high of about $744,269 in terms of market cap on the 21st of February 2014. At this peak, it was worth 0.00016 mBTC according to Cryptorush.

In late February, a campaign began to help raise funds for USMC SSGT Charlie Linville's (injured US Marine) Mount Everest climb. Support was pledged via The Heroes Project.

On the 6th of March, the official Facebook group was founded. On the 16th, the Topcoin paper wallet was introduced thanks to "topdude". On the 24th, the Topcoin merchant site (http://topswap.us) was created.

In April, Topcoin had its greatest exchange transaction volume on Mintpal. On the 14th of April, the Topcoin Android wallet became available via Google Play.

On the 6th of May, the Everest Mountain Climb was suspended until next year.

On the 4th of June, the trading exchange Mintpal moved Topcoin trading from TOP/BTC to TOP/LTC.

On the 10th of July, the trading of TOP was transferred from the BTC to LTC trading pair on Swisscex.

On the 7th of August, trading of TOP on MintPal ceased.

On the 1st of September, a new BitcoinTalk forum thread was created by "topdude". On the 3rd, TOP2 (a completely separate coin on a different blockchain) was launched. The launch of TOP2 and the specifications were determined by a poll on BitcoinTalk. One day later, the TOPSWAP program began where people could swap their TOP1 for TOP2 at a 1:1000 ratio. On the 14th, a mandatory client (V 2.1.1) was released. On the 26th, the exchange called AllCoin began trading of both BTC and LTC trading pairs. One day later, the campaign to raise funds for Charle Linville to climb Mount Everest began again. At the time, the number of TOP2 donated was 187,000 for the climb scheduled for the 28th of March 2015.

In November, the old Topcoin blockchain and network ceased to exist.

www.facebook.com/OfficialTopcoin
www.reddit.com/r/topcoin
www.twitter.com/topcoindev

OLD TOP COIN SPECIFICATION

Symbol: TOP
Algorithm: Scrypt Proof of Work
Total Coins: 11.52 billion
Block Time/Difficulty Re-target: 30 seconds/every block
Confirmations per Transaction: 4
Pre-mine: None

The Original
Topcoin Logo

Topcoin mascot thanks
to "crymzyn"

Initially it provided 1 million coins per block. The block pay out halved approximately every two days or 5,760 blocks. The minimum pay out of each block was 1 at which the network generated random bonus blocks. Each hour there was a 10X pay out block and another 100X pay out block each day.

MISCELLANEOUS

The proof of work mining for Topcoin was initially rapid with quick distribution. It took about one and a half months for the TOP block reward to reach 1 TOP.

A new version of the coin, Top2coin, was initiated as a result of the older coin becoming untenable. This was because proof of work mining eventually became unprofitable due to the network hashrate diminishing to low levels.

AntiqueJackpot.com was the first merchant to accept Topcoin as a form of payment on the 15th of March 2015.

EXCHANGES

TOP EXCHANGES

Swisscex (added on ~04/02/14)
Cryptorush (added on ~07/02/14)
AllCoin (added on ~08/02/14)
Newaltex (added on ~09/02/14)
MintPal (added on ~09/02/14)
Comkort (added on ~23/03/14)
AllCrypt (added on ~12/04/14)
Europex (added on ~21/04/14)

TOP2 EXCHANGES

Cryptex (added on ~04/09/14)
AllCoin (added on ~25/09/14)
Comkort (added on ~08/10/14)

TOP2 TEAM

"topdude" - Founder/Developer
"crymzyn" (Brandon) - Developer

TOP2

ULTRACOIN

"WELCOME TO THE FUTURE"

Scrypt-Chacha PoW/PoS Hybrid

BLOCK REWARD DISTRIBUTION SCHEDULE TABLE

Block Phase	Block Number	Reward	Date of Initial Block
Pre-mine	1	2,000,000	~31st of January 2014
Initial Phase	2-239,999	50	~1st of February 2014
Second Phase	240,000-989,999	15	~27th of April 2014
1st Halving	990,000-1,979,999	7.5	~30th of September 2015
2nd Halving	1,980,000-2,969,999	3.75	~17th of August 2017
3rd Halving	2,970,000-3,959,999	1.875	~6th of July 2019

And so on...

UTC

ULTRACOIN

"WELCOME TO THE FUTURE"

SPECIFICATION

Symbol:	UTC
Launched (Founder):	1st of February 2014 (Reggie Middleton)
Hashing Algorithm:	Scrypt-Chacha
Timestamping Algorithm:	Hybrid Proof of Work/Proof of Stake
Address Begins With:	U
Total Coins:	~100 million
Block Time/Difficulty Retarget:	30 seconds/30mins
Coins per Block:	50 Initially (see first page)
Confirmations per Transaction:	5
Pre-mine:	2% (1.6% IPO) ~2 million (1.6 million)

- The number of coins rewarded for each block halves every 990,000 blocks from the 15 block reward.

- The difficulty re-targets every 30mins.

- Mined block confirmation: 50

- NFactor Integration.

- Mined via CPU and GPU, with an ASIC resistant Scrypt ChaCha base.

- The remaining 400,000 UTC had 100,000 subtracted from it to go to development bounty's as well as some of the income from the 1.6% pre mine sold off at launch. The remaining 300,000 where split up between the creators as well as their external consultant.

- There is a weekly 0.1% PoS interest rate on coins held in a user's wallet.

http://ultracoin.net	(Official Website)
http://ultracha.in/chain/ultracoin	(Block Explorer)
http://ultracointalk.org/	(Official Forum)
http://useultracoin.com/	(Business Directory)

UTC

HISTORY

"WELCOME TO THE FUTURE"

Ultracoin was announced on Bitcointalk on the 13th of January 2014 by user "bumface" before launch on the 1st of February. Ultracoin reached an all time high of about $2,254,590 in terms of market cap on the 9th. At this peak, one UTC was worth about 71 cents (USD). On the same day, it was added to Coinmarketcap.com. Five days later, the UTC forum (forum.ultracoin.net) was launched. On the 22nd, the official UTC website (www.ultracoin.net) was born. On the 26th, the current Facebook group was created.

On the 9th of March, in a video on YouTube, 100 UTC was sent from the Netherlands to New York, from New York to Australia, and from Australia back to the Netherlands, fully confirming between each step in just 2 minutes and 31 seconds. On the 18th, each UTC was worth $0.0325 with about 14,638,227 coins in circulation. In the last week of March, altoutlet.com added Ultracoin on their site.

On the 9th of April, phase 1 of the wallet update (V 1.0.1.0) was completed. It was not mandatory but highly recommended as checkpoints were added. One day later, Ultracoin went live on the gift card site pock.io. On the 16th, the new forum (www.ultracointalk.org) was launched. On the 22nd, it was announced users had to update their wallets (V 1.0.2.0) otherwise they would remain on an old blockchain. This was necessary as it implemented a block reward reduction from 50 to 15 at block 240,000, implemented coin control and fixed issues regarding the Heartbleed bug.

On the 9th of May, a mandatory wallet update (V 1.0.3.0) became available to download and install. This update decreased loading times by 90% and introduced the stake mining checkbox. A campaign was launched on the 12th of May in order to sponsor Elsa Hammond in her attempt to row 2,400 miles from California to Hawaii. "dcgirl" joined up with BitcoinWoman Magazine to make this possible. The event occurred in Summer 2014. On the 18th, "Paulgr" of BTC-e became the Director of Strategic Partnership at Ultracoin. On the 19th, "UltraSmart" joined the Ultracoin development team. He volunteered to serve as the Ultracoin Community Leader. He refers to members of UTC as Ultracoin Community Members (UCMs).

On the 1st of June, Coinpayments.net added Ultracoin. Two days later, a super fast block explorer (ultracha.in/chain/ultracoin) was created. A mandatory wallet (V 1.0.4.0) was released on the 26th. It introduced a new weekly 0.1% PoS interest rate and the new UTC 2.0 logo onto the client interface.

On the 4th of July, it was announced that Ultracoin would change to being completely Proof of Stake. However, after taking community opinion into consideration, this was postponed indefinitely. On the 29th, the layout of the official forum was changed with the inclusion of a new chat box.

On the 6th of August, a new Bitcointalk thread was created. This coincided with the re-branding of the coin to Ultracoin 2.0.

On the 2nd of October, the directory website (http://useultracoin.com/) of businesses that accept Ultracoin as payment went live. On the 10th, Ultracoin attended the largest cryptocurrency mining conference "Hashers United" in Las Vegas.

On the 8th of December, a client was released (hard fork at block number 861,677).

www.facebook.com/ultracoinnet
www.twitter.com/official_utc
www.reddit.com/r/official_utc/

MISCELLANEOUS

Because Ultracoin is a Scrypt chacha coin, it is resistant to Scrypt ASICs.

The first Ultracoin project was thanks to @UltracoinGirl. It was a cryptocurrency arbitrage profitability calculation website called Ultra-Arb. Development continues on Ultra-Arb as they expand its functions, and create a premium subscription model.

Ultracoin is now governed by a Board of Directors, a board that will guide their efforts and ensure that they are using resources most effectively, and delivering the maximum value to their community and stakeholders.

Notable allies are "xwebnetwork" and "dcgirl" who are active in the developement of Ultracoin services and apps.

IPO was used to buy Alpha Technology Scrypt ASICS, which were bought by "bumface". This are used for passive income for the development team.

EXCHANGES

Poloniex (added on ~09/02/14)
Coinmarket (added on ~10/02/14)
Cryptorush (added on ~19/02/14)
MintPal (added on ~26/02/14)
Swisscex (added on ~26/02/14)
Comkort (added on ~02/03/14)
C-Cex (added on ~04/03/14)
OpenEx (added on ~06/03/14)
Cryptsy (added on ~07/03/14)
Bittrex (added on ~17/03/14)
AGX (added on ~25/03/14)
Bleutrade (added on ~21/04/14)
Crypto-Trade (added on ~09/05/14)
Coinnext (added on ~24/05/14)

UTC TEAM

Reggie Middleton—Founder
Steven "Rapture" - Management Director
Paul (Paulr1) - Director of Planning and Marketing
Fabian (Fabietech) - Director of Systems and Coin Development
Ming Changi Il-Suang—Director of Treasury with audit responsibility

UTC

WORLDCOIN

"THINK OUTSIDE THE BANKS"

Scrypt Proof of Work

BLOCK REWARD DISTRIBUTION SCHEDULE TABLE

Block Phase	Block Number	Reward	Date of Initial Block
First Phase	1-20,160	64	~14th of May 2013
Second Phase	20,161-40,320	63.36	~21st of May 2013
Third Phase	40,321-60,480	62.73	~28th of May 2013
Fourth Phase	60,481-80,640	62.10	~4th of June 2013
Fifth Phase	80,641-100,800	61.479	~11th of June 2013
Sixth Phase	100,801-120,960	60.86421	~18th of June 2013
Seventh Phase	120,961-141,120	60.2555679	~25th of June 2013

And so on...
The coin reward reduces by 1% each week.

WDC

WORLDCOIN

"THINK OUTSIDE THE BANKS"
"SEPARATED BY BORDERS, UNITED BY TECHNOLOGY"

SPECIFICATION

Symbol:	WDC
Launched (Founder):	14th of May 2013 4:13am (UTC) ("WorldCoin")
Hashing Algorithm:	Scrypt
Timestamping Algorithm:	Proof of Work
Address Begins With:	W
Total Coins:	265,420,800
Block Time/Difficulty Retarget:	30 seconds/120 blocks (~1 hour)
Coins per Block:	(see the first page)
Confirmations per Transaction:	2
Pre-mine:	None

- Uses the Scrypt hashing algorithm so it can be mined with CPU and GPU.

- Block target is 30 seconds so a new block is generated every 30 seconds on average

- Difficulty retargets every 120 which is roughly every hour.

- A Bitcoin descendent.

- Block reward was initially 64 coins and reduces by 1% every week (20,160 blocks).

- The Worldcoin network is protected by WorldShield which is an ongoing project to prevent disruptions and network attacks.

http://www.worldcoinalliance.net/	(Official Website)
http://coinplorer.com/WDC	(Block Explorer)
http://worldcoinforum.org/	(Official Forum)
http://crowdfund.worldcoinalliance.net/	(Crowd Funding Website)
http://www.worldcoincares.org/	(Charity Website)

WDC

HISTORY

"SEPARATED BY BORDERS, UNITED BY TECHNOLOGY"

"THINK OUTSIDE THE BANKS"

On the 14th of May 2013, user "WorldCoin" announced Worldcoin on Bitcointalk. On the 21st, Worldcoin was added to Coinmarketcap.com. Also in May, the forum (www.worldcoinforum.org) and the original official website (www.worldcoin.in) were created.

On the 29th of June, Worldcoin, Feathercoin and Phoenixcoin proposed to form a partnership in order to develop services together. This happened on the 22nd of July with the formation of UNOCS.

On the 21st of September, Cryptsy introduced the trading pair WDC/LTC.

Worldcoin reached an all time high of about $31,057,183 in terms of market cap on the 4th of December. At this peak, one WDC was worth 1.5 mBTC according to Cryptsy. On the 7th, the Worldcoin Alliance Twitter page was created. On the 10th, the first WDC/USD trading pair was added to Crypto Trade. On the 28th, the Scharmbeck Worldcoin Android wallet app was released on Google Play.

On the 5th of January 2014, www.followthecoin.com interviewed the founders of Worldcoin.

On the 15th of February, the WDC Facebook group (www.facebook.com/WorldcoinWDC) was founded.

On the 1st of March, the website www.worldcoinalliance.net went live.

On the 3rd of April, the Worldcoin Alliance released a crowdfunding platform on which users can begin and donate to a variety of projects. One project called "The Water Well in Kenya" reached its target fund. On the 4th, a new official Worldcoin subreddit (www.reddit.com/r/WorldcoinAlliance) was created. On the 14th, Worldcoin was discussed in a Yahoo Finance article (Canada).

On the 15th of May, a client (V 8.6.2) was released. It had to be installed by users before the 31st of May. It fixed issues relating to the Heartbleed Bug as well as adding advanced protection against 51% attacks.

On the 1st of June, the Worldcoin Cares charity was founded. On the 24th, the Worldcoin Cares Facebook group was created.

On the 1st of July, the Worldcoin Android wallet app was released on Google Play.

On the 14th of August, Worldcoin suffered a fork of the blockchain. Many multipools and exchanges did not update to the latest mandatory client (V 8.6.2). They remained on the previous client (V 8.6.1). This was resolved in several days without the need of a hard fork. On the 16th, Worldcoin formed a partnership with the registered charity called "World Land Trust". Also in August, "Berzeck" joined the Worldcoin Committee.

On the 13th of September, the Worldcoin Team Bios was published along with the roadmap. This roadmap sets out future proposed projects and how they are progressing.

On the 1st of November, the wallet client (V 1.0.0), also known as the "Drunk Turtle", was completed. On the 7th, the wallet client (V 1.0.0) was released. It was delayed in order to test security and stability issues.

www.facebook.com/WorldcoinWDC
www.reddit.com/r/worldcoinalliance
www.twitter.com/WDCalliance

 **WORLDCOIN**

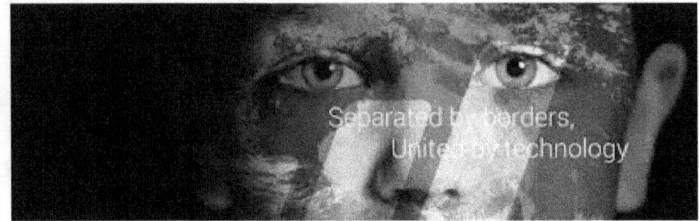

Separated by borders,
United by technology

Original Worldcoin Logo

MISCELLANEOUS

The Worldcoin Alliance represents a group of motivated Worldcoin users who decided to step up and voluntarily participate in developing, implementing and communicating Worldcoin related projects. Their members come from all over the world including the U.S., Canada, Bolivia and Australia.

Worldcoin is praised by its developers for its extremely fast transaction times, at least 20x faster than Bitcoin.

Worldcoin is a free software project released under the MIT/X11 licence which gives you the power to run, modify, copy, and to freely distribute the software at your discretion.

Worldcoin Cares (http://worldcoincares.org) was set up to forge long term relationships with global charitable organisations. A crowd funding campaign raised 30,273.34 WDC to support its creation and continued development.

EXCHANGES

Cryptsy (added on ~20/05/13)
mcxNOW (added on ~20/05/13)
Bter (added on ~20/05/13)
CoinEx (added on ~31/07/13)
PhenixEx (added on ~25/08/13)
BTC38 (added on ~09/12/13)
Crypto Trade (added on ~09/12/13)
Bittylicious (added on ~30/01/14)
Swissex (added on ~02/02/14)
Bittrex (added on ~28/02/14)
C-Cex (added on ~07/03/14)
Jubi (added on ~08/03/14)
Bleutrade (added on ~25/03/14)
Vault of Satoshi (added on ~10/04/14)
Ecoin Fund (added on ~11/04/14)
Comkort (added on ~11/04/14)
CoinNext (added on ~09/06/14)
CEX.IO (added on ~07/09/14)

WORLDCOIN COMMITTEE

Matthew Lewis (Thorgrim) (Canada) - Chairman
Johnny Beer (AcceptWorldcoins) (UK) - Public Relations
Deane Parrott (Higgson) (Australia) - Administrator
Mario Blacutt (Berzeck) (Bolivia) - Core Developer
Kevin Quasarano (Botornig) (USA) - Core Developer

WORLDCOIN ALLIANCE

Pierre-Louis Constantin (Magot) (Canada) - Developer
Jordan King (datsunking1) (USA) - Marketing
Aaron Derry (Colaxais) (UK) - Forum Moderator

 # WDC

ZETACOIN

"BUY HOLD BUILD"

SHA-256 Proof of Work

BLOCK REWARD DISTRIBUTION SCHEDULE TABLE

Block Phase	Block Number	Reward	Date of Initial Block
Initial Phase	1-80,639	1,000	~3rd of August 2013
1st Halving	80,640-161,279	500	~23rd of August 2013
2nd Halving	161,280-241,919	250	~13th of September 2013
3rd Halving	241,920-322,559	125	~4th of October 2013
—————————	—————————	—————————	————————————-
9th Halving	725,760-806,399	1.953125	~2nd of February 2014
10th Halving	806,400——	1	~17th of February 2014

ZET now has a block reward of 1 ZET every 30 seconds.

ZET

ZETACOIN

"BUY HOLD BUILD"

SPECIFICATION

Symbol:	ZET
Launched (Founder):	3rd of August 2013, 7:06 pm (UTC) ("Giskard")
Hashing Algorithm:	SHA-256
Timestamping Algorithm:	Proof of Work
Address Begins With:	Z
Total Coins:	160 million + small yearly inflation
Block Time/Difficulty Retarget:	30 seconds/every 4 blocks based on last 90 blocks
Coins per Block:	(see the first page)
Confirmations per Transaction:	7
Pre-mine:	None

◆   Based on Bitcoin 0.9.2.1 source.

◆   There was an initial coin reward of 1000 ZET via mining.

◆   Block reward halving every 80,640 blocks ceased on the 17th of February 2014.

◆   Each block now has a reward of 1 ZET.

◆   Difficulty retargets every 4 blocks based on last 90 blocks.

◆   Zetacoin passed the 160 million coin threshold. About one million coins per year will now be released. This means that there is no hard coin cap for Zetacoin, but only a slight inflation.

◆   The developers see the small inflation as a better incentive to keep the network hashing than purely transaction fees.

http://zetacoin.cc/   (Official Site)
https://coinplorer.com/ZET   (Block Explorer)
http://zetacoin.cc/forum/   (Official Forum)

ZET

HISTORY

"BUY HOLD BUILD"

On the 3rd of August 2013, "Giskard" announced the coin on Bitcointalk. In the same month, "shakezula" set up a block explorer and "pr9me" designed a preliminary coin logo. A Facebook group for Zetacoin was founded on the 27th. The first update of the Github source was implemented with a checkpoint at block 103,010 on the last day of August.

On the 10th of September, Zetacoin was added to the site Coinmarketcap.com.

In October, Zetacoin was added to the site www.coinpayments.net on which goods and services can be sold. It allows payments in Zetacoin to be processed. Another checkpoint was implemented at block 252,509 in the same month.

Zetacoin reached an all time high of about $17,665,381 in terms of market cap on the 10th of December. At this peak, one ZET was worth 0.1235 mBTC according to Cryptsy. Three days later, the original official Zetacoin forum (www.zetacoin.ace.st) was founded thanks to "dercie".

A new official website (www.zetacoin.cc) was launched on the 1st of January 2014. This website is maintained by the Zetacoin Builders Association District 305, referred to as ZBAD305. On the 7th, a new Facebook group was founded. On the 16th, a final decision was made on the correct Zetacoin coin logo to use. On the 22nd, a beta version of the current forum (http://zetacoin.cc/forum) went live. On the 25th, CoinEx added the ZET/DOGE trading pair.

On the 1st of February, the official website was translated into Czech thanks to "@MarekFortCZ". On the 12th, the Android app was supposed to be launched. It had been delayed until final adjustments were made. On the 15th, a site called "cryptr" was launched by "Konen" from ZBAD305. It is an international advertising platform built around the coin. "Giskard" announced that Zetacoin reached its inflationary phase (~0.6% per annum) as well as implementing another checkpoint on the 20th. BlueCoinStock added Zetacoin on their site at the end of the month.

On the 6th of March, an updated wallet (V 0.8.99.13) became available to download. In addition to this, the Github source and Windows build were updated. On the 28th of March, the Android wallet was released on Google Play after much anticipation.

At the beginning of April, Zetacoin increased in value by approximately 500% with the space of several days.

On the 9th of May, German State TV broadcasted a programme on which Zetacoin was featured. A YouTube video titled "Electrischer Reporter: Kryptowährung" was posted.

On the 21st of June, a wallet client (V 0.8.99.18) was released. (previous release based on Bitcoin 0.8.3)

On the 28th of July, a new Windows client and source code based on Bitcoin 0.9.2 was released.

www.facebook.com/zetacoin.cc
www.reddit.com/r/zetacoins/
www.twitter.com/zetacoincc

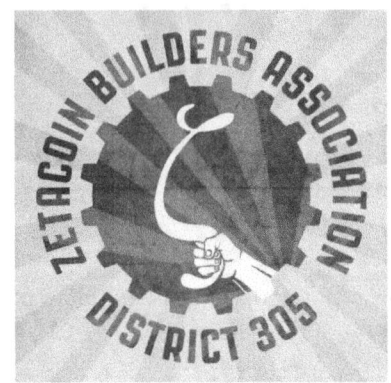

MISCELLANEOUS

Its developers site Zetacoin as being 20 times faster than Bitcoin in terms of transaction speed.

Zetacoin has a group called the ZBAD305 (Zetacoin Builders. Association District 305) who are responsible for looking after the health of the coin. This group spans many countries and its main aim is to implement and complete projects. They were founded on the 8th of December 2013.

The official website can be read in either English, German, Dutch or Czech.

ZTC was not used as the symbol of the coin due to it already being claimed by Zenithcoin.

"Giskard" donates ZET as rewards to those who help create pools, block explorers and promote the coin.

EXCHANGES

CoinEx (added on ~14/08/14)
Cryptsy (added on ~25/08/13)
Bter (added on ~27/08/13)
Coins-e (added on ~19/12/13)
MintPal (added on ~04/04/14)
Europex (added on ~04/04/14)
Swisscex (added on ~07/04/14)
Atomic-Trade (added on ~09/04/14)
AllCrypt (added on ~12/04/14)
C-Cex (added on ~17/04/14)
CoinNext (added on ~09/06/14)
RapidCX (added on ~18/06/14)
Jubi (added on ~08/07/14)
Bittrex (added on ~14/07/14)

ZET TEAM

"Giskard"—Founder

ZET

Launch Dates

DATES FROM WHICH USERS COULD MINE/MINT COINS

Cryptocurrency	Symbol	Date Launched
Bitcoin	BTC	3rd of January 2009
Litecoin	LTC	13th of October 2011
Peercoin	PPC	19th of August 2012
Feathercoin	FTC	16th of April 2013
Franko	FRK	11th of May 2013
Worldcoin	WDC	14th of May 2013
Goldcoin	GLD	15th of May 2013
Digitalcoin	DGC	20th of May 2013
Fastcoin	FST	29th of May 2013
Megacoin	MEC	1st of June 2013
Anoncoin	ANC	5th of June 2013
Infinitecoin	IFC	5th of June 2013
Crypto Bullion	CBX	28th of June 2013
Primecoin	XPM	7th of July 2013
Diamond	DMD	13th of July 2013
Quark	QRK	21st of July 2013
Hobonickels	HBN	24th of July 2013
Zetacoin	ZET	3rd of August 2013
Colossuscoin	COL	22nd of August 2013

Launch Dates

DATES FROM WHICH USERS COULD MINE/MINT COINS

Cryptocurrency	Symbol	Date Launched
Tagcoin	TAG	27th of October 2013
Nxt	NXT	24th of November 2013
Dogecoin	DOGE	8th of December 2013
Fedoracoin	TIPS	22nd of December 2013
Kittehcoin	MEOW	24th of December 2013
Mooncoin	MOON	30th of December 2013
Digibyte	DGB	12th of January 2014
Darkcoin	DRK	18th of January 2014
Leafcoin	LEAF	24th of January 2014
Saturncoin	SAT	1st of February 2014
Ultracoin	UTC	1st of February 2014
Auroracoin	AUR	2nd of February 2014
Topcoin	TOP	2nd of February 2014
Reddcoin	RDD	2nd of February 2014
Mintcoin	MINT	6th of February 2014
Maxcoin	MAX	6th of February 2014
Mazacoin	MZC	22nd of February 2014
Blackcoin	BC	24th of February 2014
Britcoin	BRIT	27th of June 2014
Saturn2coin	SAT2	30th of June 2014
Topcoin2	TOP2	3rd of September 2014

www.coinmarketcap.com

DATES WHEN EACH COIN WAS ADDED TO THIS SITE

Coin	Symbol	Date Added
Bitcoin	BTC	Unknown
Fastcoin	FST	Unknown
Litecoin	LTC	Unknown
Peercoin	PPC	Unknown
Feathercoin	FTC	9th of May 2013
Worldcoin	WDC	21st of May 2013
Digitalcoin	DGC	9th of June 2013
Franko	FRK	9th of June 2013
Goldcoin	GLD	14th of June 2013
Megacoin	MEC	7th of July 2013
Infinitecoin	IFC	10th of July 2013
Primecoin	XPM	10th of July 2013
Anoncoin	ANC	14th of July 2013
Crypto Bullion	CBX	4th of August 2013
Quark	QRK	25th of August 2013
Zetacoin	ZET	10th of September 2013
Tagcoin	TAG	5th of November 2013
Colossuscoin	COL	1st of December 2013

www.coinmarketcap.com

DATES WHEN EACH COIN WAS ADDED TO THIS SITE

Coin	Symbol	Date Added
Nxt	NXT	4th of December 2013
Dogecoin	DOGE	15th of December 2013
Diamond	DMD	18th of December 2013
Hobonickels	HBN	20th of December 2013
Lottocoin	LOT	27th of December 2013
Fedoracoin	TIPS	31st of December 2013
Mooncoin	MOON	6th of January 2014
Kittehcoin	MEOW	24th of January 2014
Leafcoin	LEAF	1st of February 2014
Digibyte	DGB	6th of February 2014
Reddcoin	RDD	9th of February 2014
Ultracoin	UTC	9th of February 2014
Maxcoin	MAX	12th of February 2014
Darkcoin	DRK	13th of February 2014
Topcoin	TOP	16th of February 2014
Mintcoin	MINT	19th of February 2014
Auroracoin	AUR	26th of February 2014
Mazacoin	MZC	26th of February 2014
Blackcoin	BC	28th of February 2014
Saturncoin	SAT	11th of March 2014
Britcoin	BRIT	3rd of July 2014

Cryptocurrency Rankings

BASED ON WWW.COINMARKETCAP.COM
(# COLUMN WAS THE RANKING OF THE COIN ON 28/07/2014 7:22PM BST)

Cryptocurrency	Symbol	Rank	Market Cap	One Coin =
Bitcoin	BTC	1	$7,633,393,540	$583.94
Litecoin	LTC	2	$231,731,679	$7.57
NXT	NXT	4	$43,501,974	$0.043502
Peercoin	PPC	5	$25,276,699	$1.17
Darkcoin	DRK	6	$23,879,200	$5.29
Dogecoin	DOGE	7	$18,088,653	$0.000204
Blackcoin	BC	11	$7,267,036	$0.097366
Reddcoin	RDD	14	$5,338,637	$0.000199
Quark	QRK	20	$2,953,341	$0.011906
Zetacoin	ZET	22	$2,738,785	$0.016992
Primecoin	XPM	24	$1,968,140	$0.299253
Feathercoin	FTC	25	$1,770,429	$0.035013
Megacoin	MEC	28	$1,278,594	$0.052114
Infinitecoin	IFC	29	$1,202,691	$0.000013
Worldcoin	WDC	37	$783,755	$0.012796
Anoncoin	ANC	42	$639,802	$0.566009
Maxcoin	MAX	45	$590,534	$0.024476
Goldcoin	GLD	48	$442,676	$0.013858
Mintcoin	MINT	53	$342,163	$0.000018

Cryptocurrency Rankings (2)

BASED ON WWW.COINMARKETCAP.COM

(# COLUMN WAS THE RANKING OF THE COIN ON 28/07/2014 7:22PM BST)

Cryptocurrency	Symbol	Rank	Market Cap	One Coin =
Digibyte	DGB	59	$232,752	$0.000188
Digitalcoin	DGC	64	$203,415	$0.012517
Ultracoin	UTC	73	$166,897	$0.009729
Crypto Bullion	CBX	79	$150,288	$0.157663
Hobonickel	HBN	82	$134,427	$0.024876
Tagcoin	TAG	92	$105,031	$0.059711
Auroracoin	AUR	102	$86,051	$0.052479
Diamond	DMD	117	$63,500	$0.123848
Fedoracoin	TIPS	119	$62,636	$2.2e-7
Mazacoin	MZC	128	$55,761	$0.000108
Saturn2coin	SAT2	159	$35,566	$0.004534
Mooncoin	MOON	164	$33,300	$2.4e-7
Fastcoin	FST	173	$28,003	$0.000318
Franko	FRK	198	$20,330	$0.070069
Topcoin	TOP	233	$8,743	$3.8e-7
Colossuscoin	COL	301	$71,025	$2.3e-7
Leafcoin	LEAF	302	$64,245	$0.000004
Kittehcoin	MEOW	323	$5,301	$3.8e-7

Bottom three coins had low volume

Cryptocurrency Rankings

BASED ON WWW.COINMARKETCAP.COM

(# COLUMN WAS THE RANKING OF THE COIN ON 12/09/2014 12PM BST)

Cryptocurrency	Symbol	Rank	Market Cap	One Coin =
Bitcoin	BTC	1	$6,307,010,168	$475.73
Litecoin	LTC	2	$170,468,932	$5.34
NXT	NXT	5	$42,539,976	$0.04254
Dogecoin	DOGE	6	$18,327,572	$0.000199
Peercoin	DRK	7	$16,184,312	$0.745360
Darkcoin	DOGE	8	$12,796,350	$2.76
Blackcoin	BC	17	$3,676,850	$0.049242
Quark	QRK	21	$1,901,932	$0.007663
Reddcoin	RDD	23	$1,832,781	$0.000067
Zetacoin	ZET	25	$1,779,242	$0.011059
Primecoin	XPM	29	$1,252,752	$0.179887
Feathercoin	FTC	31	$1,085,991	$0.019793
Maxcoin	MAX	35	$928,682	$0.025923
Worldcoin	WDC	39	$782,773	$0.012188
Infinitecoin	NVC	42	$731,888	$0.000008
Megacoin	MEC	43	$731,839	$0.02905
Anoncoin	ANC	54	$503,082	$0.406319
Mintcoin	MINT	68	$312,254	$0.000016
Goldcoin	GLD	76	$238,813	$0.007376

Cryptocurrency Rankings (2)

BASED ON WWW.COINMARKETCAP.COM

(# COLUMN WAS THE RANKING OF THE COIN ON 12/09/2014 12PM BST)

Cryptocurrency	Symbol	Rank	Market Cap	One Coin =
Hobonickels	HBN	91	$163,926	$0.026593
Digitalcoin	DGC	92	$154,847	$0.009132
Digibyte	DGB	93	$149,205	$0.000102
Ultracoin	UTC	98	$136,154	$0.007501
Crypto Bullion	CBX	105	$123,640	$0.129588
Auroracoin	AUR	116	$92,506	$0.051313
Tagcoin	TAG	139	$68,475	$0.035033
Mooncoin	MOON	151	$56,776	$3.2e-7
Colossuscoin	COL	162	$50,084	$1.6e-7
Britcoin	BRIT	166	$46,700	$0.004314
Fedoracoin	TIPS	169	$45,909	$1.6e-7
Diamond	DMD	173	$41,868	$0.071351
Fastcoin	FST	178	$39,931	$0.000431
Mazacoin	MZC	183	$36,200	$0.000066
Leafcoin	LEAF	227	$18,801	$0.000001
Kittehcoin	MEOW	238	$14,731	$9.6e-7
Saturn2coin	SAT2	240	$14,126	$0.001795
Franko	FRK	245	$12,559	$0.043287
Topcoin2	TOP2	???	???	???